Reducing the Risk, Increasing the Promise

Strategies for Student Success

Sherrel Bergmann
and
Judith Allen Brough

EYE ON EDUCATION
6 DEPOT WAY WEST, SUITE 106
LARCHMONT, NY 10538
(914) 833–0551
(914) 833–0761 fax
www.eyeoneducation.com

Library of Congress Cataloging-in-Publication Data

Bergmann, Sherrel.
    Reducing the risk, increasing the promise : strategies for student success
/ Sherrel Bergmann and Judy Brough.
    p. cm.
 ISBN 978-1-59667-194-2
1. School failure—Prevention. 2. Motivation in education. I. Brough,
Judith Allen. II. Title.
    LB3063.B47 2011
    371.2′85—dc23   2011023522

Sponsoring Editor: Robert Sickles
Production Editor: Lauren Davis
Copyeditor: Elayne Masters
Designer and Compositor: Rick Soldin
Cover Designer: Dave Strauss, 3FoldDesign

Also Available from Eye On Education

Teach My Kid—I Dare You!
The Educator's Essential Guide to Parent Involvement
Sherrel Bergmann, Judith Allen Brough, and David Shepard

Teach Me—I Dare You!
Judith Allen Brough, Sherrel Bergmann, and Larry C. Holt

Lead Me—I Dare You!
Managing Resistance to School Change
Sherrel Bergmann and Judith Allen Brough

Dropout Prevention Fieldbook:
Best Practices from the Field
Franklin P. Schargel

152 Ways to Keep Students in School:
Effective, Easy-to-Implement Tips for Teachers
Franklin P. Schargel

Reaching the Wounded Student
Joe Hendershott

Battling Boredom:
99 Strategies to Spark Student Engagement
Bryan Harris

What Do You Say When…:
Best Practices for Improving Student Behavior
Hal Holloman and Peggy H. Yates

From At-Risk to Academic Excellence:
What Successful Leaders Do
Franklin P. Schargel, Tony Thacker, and John S. Bell

Helping Students Motivate Themselves:
Practical Answers to Classroom Challenges
Larry Ferlazzo

About the Authors

Dr. Sherrel Bergmann has listened carefully to teachers and at-risk students her entire career as a teacher, counselor, parent, consultant, university dean, and professor. What she heard and experienced with these students and teachers motivated her to write this book and the activities in it. She is a Lounsbury Award winner from the National Middle School Association and has been recognized with many awards from the National Association of Secondary School Principals, The Association of Illinois Middle Schools, and the Connecticut Association of Principals for her leadership, publications, and presentations. She is a tireless advocate for students who could fall through the cracks if there were not someone there to catch them.

Dr. Judith Allen Brough is Professor Emerita, Gettysburg College, Gettysburg, PA. She is an award-winning teacher and advocate for children, especially for young adolescents and those students who are labeled "at-risk." Her numerous publications and presentations offer practical strategies based solidly in educational theory, research, and experience. She has held leadership positions for the National Middle School Association (now called the Association for Middle Level Education), the National Association of Secondary School Principals, and the Association for Supervision and Curriculum Development. Her professional interest lies in motivating administrators, teachers, future teachers, and students to bring joy and meaningful work into every classroom.

Contents

Free Downloads

Some of the activities discussed and displayed in this book are also available on Eye On Education's Web site as Adobe Acrobat files. Permission has been granted to purchasers of this book to download these resources and print them.

You can access these downloads by visiting Eye On Education's Web site: www.eyeoneducation.com. Click FREE DOWNLOADS or search or browse our Web site to find this book, and then scroll down for downloading instructions.

You'll need your book buyer access code: RTR-7194-2

Index of Downloads

Foreword

This book is dedicated to those teachers and administrators who go to school every day eager to teach and come home frustrated because of kids at all ages and stages who simply don't seem to want to learn. Just when the educators seem to be making progress, the students move, have a home crisis, or get in trouble at school. They feel that they have no control over the outside baggage that the students bring to school. As teachers spend more and more time on these students, others who are barely achieving fall into the at-risk group because they, too, need teacher attention. Teachers and administrators find they are spending 80 percent of their time on 20 percent of their students. While they never give up on the kids, stress levels increase as the school year progresses.

Teachers who are not willing to leave a child behind need support and encouragement to continue their daily interactions with these students. When they ask for help, they do not ask for materials or money or time. They need help finding ways to encourage students to be respectful, resilient, responsible, and resourceful. What they want are attitudes and behaviors from their students that enable the entire class to make progress and develop their talents as learners, a goal that can be achieved by teaching students to develop positive classroom relationships and reading skills. They often encounter students who have none of these skills or are seriously lacking in most of them.

This book is a compilation of the best ideas we have used and those we have learned from teachers and administrators who have successfully helped at-risk students thrive. All of the techniques can be used individually, but they are most effective when used in concert and spread over the school year as a daily classroom component. The parent strategies are designed to be shared with parents by teachers and the administration and even used as special topics for parent workshops.

The real key to using this book is to develop a proactive approach to cultivating these skills in all students. Respect, responsibility, resourcefulness, and resilience are too often abstract terms for students who do not have a frame of reference for what those behaviors look like. Perhaps the most important *R* for teachers is *Recognition*. When teachers or parents recognize the need for students to develop these skills, they can then use the strategies and lessons in this book, model the skills in the classroom or home, and watch students turn from at risk to at promise.

Who Are These Students and Why Should We Listen to Them?

Recently a teacher asked her colleagues for help with a student. It seems that this student did not want to come to school, refused to do any work, and was falling behind. He was destined to fail if his current attitude prevailed. When the counselor and principal talked to him, he said," Just go ahead and suspend me. Then I won't have to come to school."

Select the grade level that you believe this student to be in:

12th grade

10th grade

8th grade

4th grade

2nd grade

The answer is 2nd grade, but it could have been any of the other grades also. The challenge of keeping kids in school starts much earlier than it did even ten years ago, and the difficulties are often compounded by absent parents, poverty, boredom, substance abuse, special needs that have not been identified, and a variety of other social issues that students face.

Why is it that two students come to school from the same home, same family, and one has success and the other fails? Is it because one was born with more ability? Is it because one is a girl and one a boy? Is it a set of special teachers that one is assigned? Is it that they have moved among several schools at least six times in eight years, and one child is better able to adapt than the other? Is it that one is physically healthy while the other has persistent allergies? Is it that one makes friends easily and the other is a bully? Is it that by seventh grade, one kept trying but the other gave up?

What is it that makes some kids more resilient, respectful, resourceful, and responsible than others? What helps students learn to read productively, use their talents, and develop positive relationships? This book examines those developmental skills as they pertain to at-risk students. These students are also at-promise because most of them know what skills they need from school. If they had help in developing those skills, they would not be labeled at-risk.

Keeping kids in school is a challenge in almost every school. While most children come to school, adapt to the routine, and adjust to the social culture, there are always a few who would rather be somewhere else. As they move through the grade levels, they find ways to beat the system and disrupt other students, and they often take more of a teacher's time than the rest of the students combined.

When teams of teachers have an opportunity to discuss students who are having learning problems and/or are causing behavioral difficulties in the classroom, they find themselves talking about the same five to ten children. They combine their efforts to help those children and find that those children are still the same ones being talked about by their teachers the next year. As those children become adolescents, their learning problems and behavioral difficulties escalate until the students become serious problems in the school or drop out either physically or emotionally.

This book is about how those students wish to be taught and what they say schools need to provide to keep them there. It is about how they start school, why they have problems, how educators and parents can help them, and what type of lessons they would like to see offered by the school. This should not require an expensive or elaborate set of lessons and strategies, but it may necessitate a systemic change in how we look at these students. As their needs are often a combination of six developmental tasks that have not been met by the system or their family environment, it is best to look at them as individuals. They have been labeled as students who lack resilience, have few positive relationships, have little self-respect, are not responsible, have minimal to no reading skills, feel they have nothing to contribute to the world, and do not have the resourcefulness to survive in school. Teachers describe them as unmotivated, irresponsible, disrespectful, unruly, disinterested, hopeless, helpless, disruptive, and unable to do what their peers can do.

In kindergarten, these children are identifiable because they do not play well with others, cannot understand the daily routine, and do not have the readiness skills to begin reading.

Students often use those same words to describe themselves. One sixth-grade male entered the school counselor's office the first day of school and stated, "I wanted you to meet me before someone sends me here. I will probably be spending a lot of time with you." What he was lacking in self-esteem and respect, he made up for with resourcefulness.

Transition skills are essential to human survival but often lacking in at-risk kids. They must learn how to adapt to new environments and new expectations. Each of the following chapters provides strategies that have been used successfully to help children of all ages stay in school and learn.

Combined, the chapters offer a formal or informal curriculum that can be adapted as a whole or in part by teachers, administrators, and parents. Interviews with hundreds of teachers and students for this book have offered several consistent findings:

- Girls and boys need to be approached and assisted differently to keep them in school.

- Teachers find that they spend nearly 80 percent of their time on 20 percent of their students. They would like to offer the intense assistance that these students require to all of their students.

- There are strategies, experiences, and attitudes that do make a difference in the lives of these kids.

- The more parents are involved in their children's education, the more those children are apt to stay in school and do well.

- The six Rs in this book must all be in place for students to survive. The absence of even one can cause students to want to remove themselves from the schooling process.

Students who were interviewed for this book offered specific suggestions regarding what schools can do to keep them there and help them learn. Here are some of their suggestions:

1. Don't call on me to read aloud when you know I do not read well.

2. Don't do the same thing all class period.

3. Read to us. Let us know how words are supposed to sound.

4. Summarize often.

5. Make me set goals.

6. Show me how to get information.

7. Find out what I know as well as what I do not know.

8. Listen to me. Let me tell you what kind of help I need.

9. Find me a mentor.

10. Find out what *does* motivate me.

11. Help me find information about life issues.

12. Let me build things.

13. Give me time to do homework in school.

14. Give me tasks that make me feel like I have accomplished something (more writing, fewer worksheets).

15. Expect me to achieve.

16. Be fair and don't escalate my mistakes.

17. Separate me from other kids until I get my work made up.

18. Let me make choices in how I learn.

19. Communicate with other adults in my life.

Case Study: Off to a "Rocky" Start

So when do these kids start to have problems and what can be done? Consider the following student.

> It all starts early for a kid like Rocky. After his first day in a preschool program for four-year-olds, the other kids can talk about only him and how the teacher had to ask him to sit down, lie down for rest time, put toys away, stop hitting other kids, clean up after lunch, listen, and not take other kids' things. One little girl said, "All the teacher did all day was talk to Rocky."
>
> Rocky's mom is very happy to have him at school all day. Her patience with Rocky's energy level is running on empty. What happens to kids like Rocky who start school before they are ready? The paths they take and their school success depends on numerous variables including the ability to develop resilience, respect, responsibility, resourcefulness, reading skills, and relationships with peers. How they respond to intervention, to teachers, to other students, and to the routine process of schooling makes a significant difference in whether or not they decide to stay in school and learn.
>
> Rocky most likely enters kindergarten as a young five-year-old and maintains the same level of energy and lack of attention that he had in preschool. His teacher tries a variety of physical classroom activities to keep his interest. Other children laugh at his antics, and he finds he gets attention by not following the routine. While he may be intellectually capable, he may not apply his intellect in order to progress at a normal rate. The teacher probably recommends him for retention at the end of the year.
>
> By third grade, Rocky is falling further behind the other kids. He has been tested, labeled, and medicated for attention deficit disorder. He begins to feel like he is not like the other kids and tries to maintain his peer status by making fun of others and bullying smaller children. His peers no longer think his antics are funny, as he constantly disturbs them at work. The teachers try numerous interventions with little success. They keep passing him with recommendations for placement in special education in the next grade.

As Rocky begins middle school and puberty, he feels out of control of his body and his actions. He understands the content of his classes but cannot seem to complete the assigned work, hand it in when he does do it, or ask for help. He does not qualify for special education because he is academically competent. He can do the work but won't. He spends a lot of time in the middle school resource room and finds he can talk easily to the resource room teacher. This teacher understands him, and that connection helps him stay focused and productive. He passes the eighth grade with adequate grades and high scores on state achievement tests.

At the end of eighth grade, Rocky asks his parents if he has to go to high school. They tell him that he must complete school. Even though he decides to give high school a try, an antagonistic relationship begins between them. What happens during his transition to high school will either make or break Rocky as a student and an adult.

During ninth grade, Rocky is interviewed by his counselor and encouraged to try out for football and take classes in the technology program. To participate in those programs, he must maintain his grades and attend all classes. He starts school with a desire to participate, makes some progress in his academic work, and gets to play on the freshman football team. Football helps his relationship with his parents, who now see him as having a talent and some success. When football season is over, he is given a chance to be the assistant in the technology lab. He enjoys the work and has respect for the teacher. He sets a goal to get good grades so he can go to college and get a good job in the computer field.

OR

During the ninth grade transition, the counselors and administrators look at his record and place Rocky in basic classes for students with academic difficulties. No one actually talks to Rocky and his parents about high school. He is placed in classes where he receives more of the information that he already knows. He is academically competent and his boredom escalates due to his placement. He does not know how to advocate for himself and believes he has no option but to stay in the boring classes. He makes the football team but does not get to play as much as he would like. He asks the counselor to let him take technology classes but finds out that he must take the other state requirements before he can fit them into his schedule. The other students in his low-track classes have found ways to alleviate the boredom by using drugs and alcohol. They invite him to parties both on weekends and during the school day. His truancy increases with his substance abuse. His parents receive frequent calls from the school regarding his absences and behavior. He does not see himself with a future. He likes hanging with his friends instead of learning history. His talents in technology go untapped.

For all of the Rockys in our schools, the disruptive behavior, chronic truancy, and lack of academic progress are calls for help. The school must deal with those cries for help by working with the parents.

The Parents' Role in Keeping Kids in School

Schools must not underestimate the impact that parents have in developing children's attitudes towards school. Keeping kids in school starts before they actually set foot in a school. The parents' attitude toward their own school experience sets the tone for children as they develop from infancy to early childhood. Some parents tell their small children that when they get older they *have* to go to school, while others tell them that they *get* to go to school. The word *have* or *get* stays with the child as he or she enters preschool and kindergarten. Parents who do not believe that school is essential might either not enter their four-year-olds in preschool or not send them if there is the slightest inconvenience. There is a distinct difference between the parents who know that their children are not ready for school and those who know the children are ready but refuse to send them.

The four-year-old who says, "Mommy lets me stay home to watch TV when I don't want to come here" provides a strong clue to that student's future success as a student. As those children enter the social setting of preschool, parental support for the schooling process is evident. The kids who are allowed to stay home to watch TV begin a 12-year battle with the system. The attitude that school is not important causes conflict for young children who actually like school when they start but receive no support at home. Those who insist on going to school develop a set of skills that will enhance their resilience as they grow. However, children who give in to the attitude are at a greater risk of falling further and further behind and becoming chronic truants and rebellious troublemakers for teachers who attempt to enforce school policy.

The same problem is evident when children who have not attended preschool enter kindergarten. Transition becomes a key variable in student school success. The ease or difficulty of the transition from home to preschool, from preschool to kindergarten, from elementary to middle school, from middle school to high school, and from high school to either college or post high-school jobs can seriously affect students' attitudes toward themselves and their school participation. The strategies that teachers use the first week of school may make the difference in children's attitudes for the remainder of their school years.

The Impact of Transition on These Students

Consider the transition comfort levels of schooling provided during transition in these two classrooms. Both are kindergartens.

Teacher 1 is a no-nonsense teacher who provides a desk for each student, a hanger for their coats, and colorful bulletin boards. The goal of this teacher is to prepare students for first grade. On the first day of school, they learn the rules and begin working on letters and numbers.

Teacher 2 has baked a gingerbread man and tells the students as they enter the classroom that the gingerbread man has run away. Their job is to go and find the gingerbread man. First they go to the coatroom to look for the gingerbread man and hang up their coats. Second, they go to the bathrooms and knock on the doors to see if he is there. Next they go to the nurse's office to see if he has been there, and she gives them all colorful Band-Aids to put in their desks for an emergency. They leave the nurse's office and go to the library to ask if he has been there. While there, they meet the person who will help them in the library. As they leave the library, they meet the school principal, who welcomes them and tells them that the gingerbread man may be in the gym. When they go to the gym, they meet their gym teacher, who tells them about the fun things they will be doing and that he saw the gingerbread man in the cafeteria a few minutes ago. The children are led to the cafeteria where they find the gingerbread man, and enjoy him as their morning snack. Finally, they go back to the classroom where the teacher asks them about the places they have visited and the people they have met. After reviewing all the places the children will be going in the school, they read the gingerbread man story.

Transition to Middle School

The sixth-grade teacher is the homeroom teacher for 28 students. While the sixth graders have had a brief orientation to the middle school last spring and have been in the building for registration, they have not had to interact with older students until now. Many are fearful; most are apprehensive. They will now have five teachers each day instead of a single classroom teacher.

Teacher 1 takes their pictures as they enter the classroom and gives them a welcoming handshake. As soon as the class is settled, she hands out a treasure hunt that requires students to find someone in that homeroom who fits the criteria listed. They must ask each other questions and get acquainted. She joins in the treasure hunt, and they soon learn that she likes cats and has been to South America. When the treasure hunt is complete, she shows them a chart above their lockers that tells how to open a lock. They practice opening their locks and put their supplies and coats away.

Teacher 2 waits while the students struggle with their locks, puts them in assigned seats, and then reads the school handbook to them. She tells them to practice opening a lock at home because they will be marked tardy if they cannot open them the next day and are late for class.

Transition to High School

There is no homeroom in ninth grade, so the first teacher students meet is the teacher of their first class.

Teacher 1 welcomes incoming freshmen with a pretest of the content covered in the first grading period. The teacher does not ask students their names.

Teacher 2 welcomes incoming freshmen with a get-acquainted activity and overview of the entire course. The teacher has students write what they already know about the subject and spends the first day making sure all are comfortable in the class. Near the end of class, the teacher gives them a fact sheet about the high school and asks if there are any questions about the school.

Teacher 3 tells incoming freshmen that this is not middle school and that they had better get ready for a tough year, and then lets them do whatever they want.

The transition activities at each level may be make-it or break-it activities for students who are considering dropping out either physically or emotionally. Students who frequently were sent to the office for discipline infractions stated that they often felt like no one knew they were there or cared. Students stay in school when someone in school cares that they are there and lets them know that. To succeed and stay in school, students need assistance developing a set of skills that include respect for self and others, resilience, recognition of talent, responsibility, reading competence, and resourcefulness.

Often teachers find teaching those skills and still meeting all of the state curriculum requirements to be an impossible task. They face insurmountable odds today with students who, like Rocky, may be lagging two to three years behind their peers, do not want to be in school, and have little support at home and more success on the street. Many teachers say they can recognize students who are posturing to drop out by the end of fourth grade. Twenty years ago these students were classified and researched as they entered high school, but today they are being identified as early as preschool. Those who enter the school system with involved parents have a greater chance of success. Parents must be willing to work with the school and within the family to help students develop the skills that will help them succeed in school and beyond.

Abraham Maslow researched basic human needs and developed a hierarchy that is useful to teachers, administrators, and parents. (See Figure 1.1.) His basic premise is that people must first have their basic needs met in order to become a fully functioning person. Students who have enough to eat, a place to sleep, clean clothing, and no violence in their home have an advantage that increases exponentially as they age and go through the schooling process. Transience, poverty, abuse, neglect, lack of parental involvement, natural disasters, and a host of other social problems create a climate of risk that often outweighs what the school offers students. If students cannot move from one level of Maslow's Hierarchy to another, they will most likely leave school.

Two essential elements cited in the Southern Regional Education Board research report are a sense of belonging and remedial help in the early grades (Dunne, 2006). Schools with lower dropout rates have advisors that

Figure 1.1 **Maslow's Hierarchy of Needs**

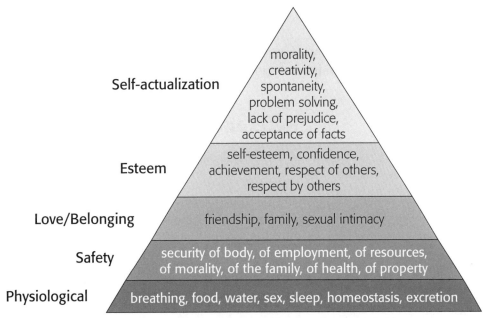

Self-actualization — morality, creativity, spontaneity, problem solving, lack of prejudice, acceptance of facts

Esteem — self-esteem, confidence, achievement, respect of others, respect by others

Love/Belonging — friendship, family, sexual intimacy

Safety — security of body, of employment, of resources, of morality, of the family, of health, of property

Physiological — breathing, food, water, sex, sleep, homeostasis, excretion

Source: Maslow's Hierarchy of Needs. Retrieved from google.com 1/28/11. Labeled for reuse.

stay with a group of students throughout their school experience. Other successful schools have on-going transition programs that help students adjust to elementary, middle and high school.

Administrators and teachers cannot assume that students who enter their school are comfortable, connected, or capable. Accurate identification of at-risk students allows teachers to teach survival skills and administer the necessary curriculum and remediation. Too often, records may not indicate a problem with acceptance, resilience, reading, truancy, or language deficiency. So many students move so often that their records do not catch up with them and the school is never really sure about the child's abilities or home situation. If parents dropped out of school, live in poverty, or are single parents, their children's risk level in school increases significantly. Not all students who are at risk come from difficult home situations. Some suffer from physical or mental handicaps that cause them to fall behind and feel like they cannot catch up. Teachers sometimes refer to those who have difficulties but are not quite failing as gray-area kids. These kids have below average grades, have several problems, and lack the skills to be (or feel) successful. Without intervention, it is easy for them to drop out of school emotionally, academically, and physically. These are the kids with two strikes against them when they come into the classroom. Today, more than ever, it has become the teacher's job to teach at-risk students how to be successful and survive.

At the most basic level, schools attempt to provide a safe and secure environment where students can learn and feel a sense of belonging. However, they cannot move a student towards self-actualization without the coopera-tion of the student, the family, and the community. Schools with a mission to create an island of decency for kids who live in a society that is not always conducive to positive growth often develop both a formal and an informal curriculum to teach and reinforce skills. The chapters that follow discuss these skills and how to help students develop them.

References

Dunne, D. (2006) Education world: School issues and education news: Strate-gies for keeping kids in school. Retrieved December 1, 2010, at www.educationworld.com/a_issues/issues/issues 120.shtml

Maslow, A. (1954). Motivation and personality. New York: Harper

2

Helping Students Develop
RESILIENCE

*"In order to succeed, people need a sense of self-efficacy,
to struggle together with resilience to meet the inevitable
obstacles and inequities of life."*

Albert Bandura

What Is Resilience?

Resilience is the ability to cope with the stresses in life as well as the ability to prepare for adversity by developing confidence, competence, and empathy. Observable in the classroom, the hallway, the bus stop, and at home, resilience is something everyone needs and most people learn. However, some have such a difficult time in life that they need to be exposed to instances requiring resilience and be supported while they develop it. Resilience is fostered through positive connections with others and successful completion of tasks. By teaching coping skills, relaxation techniques, and stress relievers, teachers and parents can help students develop resilient behaviors. Researchers (see, for example, Winfield, 1994) agree that the characteristics of resilient children include the following:

- ◆ positive peer interactions

- ◆ numerous social skills

- ◆ sensitivity

- ◆ intelligence

- ◆ a sense of humor

- ◆ empathy

- problem-solving skills

- low levels of defensiveness and aggression

- high degrees of cooperation, participation, and emotional stability

- belief that they have control over their environment, self, and life

- positive self-esteem (p. 38)

Resilient children also have parents and families who are involved in the school, who know their children's interests, and who help direct everyday tasks that their children encounter.

Because resilience is not a static characteristic, but one that is dependent on events over which students often have little control, it is difficult to classify students as resilient or not. Historically, schools have employed a deficit model in response to the lack of resilience in students rather than a proactive model that helps students develop it. There is no workbook of resilience skills. Schools and families must work together to establish a process that enables students to manage their levels of stress and to negotiate the risks involved. This process requires teachers and parents to consider how they view students who face stress. There must be a system-wide longitudinal recognition of children as at-promise instead of at-risk. School boards and administrators must understand these issues and set policies that support the process of promoting resilience skills. As students face stressful situations, educators can model, teach, recognize, and support resilient responses and behaviors.

What the Experts Say About Resilience

Authors who have studied resilience in high-risk children often define it as a set of skills that help individuals adapt and mature despite risk and adversity. Most agree that people are born with a capacity for resilience that includes a conscience, a sense of purpose, autonomy, problem-solving skills, and social skills. However, the ability to develop resilience can be delayed or limited by poverty, war, abuse, neglect, family mobility, and illness. Researchers also agree that the interaction between people's characteristics and the environment affects their resilience.

Resilience Is Observable in Each Area of Child Development

Physical Resilience

Bike riding, skating, gymnastics, and swimming are just a few of the sports that require physical resilience. Imagine trying to participate in any of those sports without some basic instruction, the right equipment, feedback, and a person to support your efforts.

Children who are born with physical handicaps and who must work to keep up with their peers are excellent role models for at-risk kids who have not developed resilience skills. Hearing-impaired children who perform in theater productions are a classic example of physical resilience. Special Olympics events provide a clear display of resilience in action. For many children with multiple handicaps, just getting up, getting dressed, and going to school each day requires the ability to deal with and move beyond life's challenges. The school system must be a rewarding environment for them to want to persevere.

Many schools start the day with an opportunity for physical activity, providing students with a boost for coping with the stresses of the school day. Resilience also helps healthy children deal with stress. Proper nutrition, adequate sleep, and regular exercise help students meet the challenges of their lives.

Emotional Resilience

Emotional resilience is the ability to overcome fear, anger, frustration, worry, loss, loneliness, and other strong emotions by using a set of positive coping skills. Preschool students who do not want to leave their parent in the morning can develop the resilience to do so if the school is a welcoming and fun place to go. Angry teens can channel anger into positive action when adults guide them through that process. The abilities to make friends, keep friends, and deal with peer rejection are all observable activities requiring emotional resilience. Student mobility rates in large city schools are very high where students often move from school to school because of the cost of rent, parental stress, or the availability of welfare services. To keep and maintain a support base, students who come from a stressful home must have the capacity to empathize with peers, find alternative ways to connect with peers, and seek support within the school system. Mobility is just one of the issues that creates a need for emotional resilience that teachers observe every day. Students who look or dress differently from the norm are often targeted by bullies. Students who are overweight are taunted and teased as early as preschool. If the students' coping mechanism is eating, then the development of resilience is thwarted. Older students learn to fight back verbally, and some resort to violence to make up for their lack of resilience. When emotional situations are life threatening, such as gang involvement, drug abuse, or violent home life, then the school must intervene with the help of community services to help build resilience in students.

Social Resilience

Social resilience starts early when children cannot find a friend to eat lunch with, are the last chosen for playground games, or cannot invite a friend to their house because their parents are drunk or abusive. Students' lack of social resilience may exist before they begin school if they have encountered abuse and neglect.

According to Taylor (1991), first-grade students should be able to control their emotions, postpone gratification, respond to social norms, and come to school in a positive frame of mind. While these are essential skills for all humans, the critical factor is how the teacher responds to the lack of these developmental characteristics. If teachers respond favorably in spite of the children's lack of development, the children will learn to see school as a socially accepting environment. If the teachers' expectations are too rigid or unaccepting, the children will face increased risk. Cultural and language differences can also affect the children's social acceptance in the school.

Some students who suffer from a lack of social skills retreat into the safety of solitude. They quit seeking friends, do not get involved in school, and often do not even talk to adults. Others keep trying until they find someone who accepts them. Schools that offer a variety of opportunities for students to build and display their talents provide for the development of social resilience, as students feel affirmed by participating in something that they share with others.

Schools provide a consistent culture for the development of social resilience. The classroom may be the safest, cleanest, and most comfortable place a child has to go. However, if the peer group does not accept a child, then that student may avoid school altogether and seek shelter elsewhere during the school day.

By the time children enter kindergarten, they understand the social norms of their home and perhaps their neighborhood. They recognize rules and can behave in familiar situations. Children come to school from parallel universes where their skills and knowledge are sufficient, and perhaps even more than adequate in their home environment, but do not match the teachers' expectations.

Social resilience develops when children merge their home social expectations with those of the school or when the school can connect the child's existing social skills to those of the home. For example: One team of seventh-grade teachers was baffled by a sudden drop in grades for 60 percent of the students. They found that students were failing quizzes or tests given in each subject on Friday. In addition, students did not turn in homework on Fridays, and the kids seemed out of sync. Once teachers asked students to write about what they did on Thursday night, they realized that they had to change their expectations to deal with the community's social norm. An unusually high number of students on that team, more than 60 percent, came from divorced families. A local custody judge had determined that Thursday would be the weekday for noncustodial parent visitation because it disrupted less of the week and offered children more consistency. When they went to visit their noncustodial parent, they had fun. And when teachers moved the tests and quizzes from Friday to a different day of the week, the scores and grades improved. The children were trying to develop the social resilience to deal with a situation over which they had no control.

In elementary schools, children often share things at school that made their whole family laugh the night before, like an off-color joke. As they tell the joke to peers and their teacher, others do not find the joke appropriate. How this is handled by teachers may affect those students' willingness to share in class for their entire school career.

Intellectual Resilience

Intellectual resilience is the ability to keep trying to learn something that is difficult. Multiplication tables, long division, state capitals, and spelling words can befuddle many students, but resilient students keep trying until they either learn them, learn how to access help, or take advantage of help that is offered. Low intellectual resilience is common in students who are two to three years behind their peers in reading and math skills when they get to middle school. They start to give up and feel that they can never catch up. Students who have given up may find success in unacceptable social practices and also compromise their social and emotional resilience.

Moral Resilience

Moral resilience is the ability to do the right thing despite temptations and motivations. Students learn early to follow school rules, but students with low moral resilience find ways to beat the system. Moral resilience requires that students know that there is right and wrong behavior, when and where to seek help, and how to remove themselves from an immoral situation. A seventh-grade girl who knows that her friends are cyber-bullying a new girl at the school recognizes that it is wrong and finds a way to get help. A fifth-grade student who continually is pressured to take drugs consistently says no. Moral resilience encourages students to help others by participating in community-service projects. Students need to understand the consequences of unethical decisions and put themselves in the shoes of others. Building sympathy and empathy and a growing sense of civic responsibility help youngsters make the "right" decisions even when no one is watching.

How Students Develop Resilience

Resilience is necessary when children's lives become imbalanced by unanticipated stressors such as loss of a loved one, exposure to violence, illness, change in family structure, natural disasters, and chronic abuse. As early as preschool, children display stressful regressive behaviors that are indicators of their lack of resilience. Resilient children recognize the stressor, respond emotionally, think about what they can do to regain balance, and then take some action, such as seeking adult help. All children need a place to escape to and people to act as their safety net. When stressors are compounded, as often happens in a natural disaster, and the adults are also trying to cope, even the most resilient child or adolescent can develop problems.

Resilience implies the ability to function under stress and to recover from setbacks and adversity. However, our children are experiencing greater rates of depression with each generation. According to Goldstein (2009), there are three indicators of resilience:

- ◆ a temperament that elicits positive response from others
- ◆ family relationships that promote trust, autonomy, initiative, and connections
- ◆ community support systems that reinforce self-esteem and self-efficacy (p. 1).

Children with learning disabilities are especially vulnerable to delayed development of resilience. The problem is compounded for children who lack language, motor, memory, or other basic skills and live in poverty or with an abusive family, lose a family member, or move frequently.

Are girls more resilient than boys? Perhaps the answer lies in how they respond to major stress. Experienced teachers and counselors who have observed children experiencing stress state that while boys tend to act out, girls seek help from friends and adults or turn inward.

Boys often display their anger and frustration outwardly; girls, especially in elementary school, tend to withdraw or talk to their friends. That is not to say that boys do not withdraw or become depressed, as many teenage boys do, or that girls do not act out their anger. As one middle-school counselor observed, girls who are stressed often discuss the issue with their peers and then go in groups to the counselor's office. Boys, on the other hand, try to stop by when no one is looking and are reluctant to open up about the issue. Many times, boys convey anger by engaging a teacher in a power struggle. Unless the teacher understands the underlying cause of the student anger, the struggle escalates and the student does poorly in the class.

Dr. Kenneth Ginsburg (2006) outlines the seven Cs of resilience for parents and teachers. His seven components are competence, confidence, connection, character, contribution, coping, and control (see www.healthychildren.org). While Ginsburg works with parents and teaches them to use the seven Cs when working with their own children, his methods can be easily adapted to the classroom.

Children develop resilience by watching resilient adults and peers. They develop it by reading about resilient people in history and current events. They develop it by talking about coping skills in class and meeting in small support groups. They develop it by learning where to go to meet their basic needs of food and shelter.

Rutter (1987) developed a useful set of criteria for administrators, teachers, and communities who wanted to develop a protective environment for students. Policy makers can examine their current curriculum and school environment to determine if they include the following processes, which foster resilience:

♦ reducing negative outcomes by changing the child's exposure to risk

♦ reducing escalation of the risk following risk exposure

♦ establishing and maintaining the child's movement towards positive self-esteem and self-efficacy

♦ opening up opportunities

Along with breakfast and free-lunch programs, referrals to community shelters and social services reduce the exposure to risk for children who enter classrooms with their basic needs unmet. One middle-school principal had a "random" drawing every week for ten students to receive new

T-shirts donated by a local radio station. Students were informed quietly by the principal that they had won the drawing and could come to the office and pick up their prize. The winners always included at least three students who needed clean clothing.

Many kindergarten teachers reduce children's exposure to risk by having a rocking chair or a place in the classroom within the teacher's sight where children can be alone to think and calm down. Children develop resilience by knowing that there is one safe place in the classroom and/or school where they can always go for help or to think.

One creative elementary school teacher had great success with a cardboard refrigerator box that the students decorated and decided was their "alone-time reading room." The teacher cut several strategically placed windows and doors in the box so she could see the students. A soft rug was placed on the floor and the box placed over it. Spending time in the room was a reward, not a punishment. Students could earn the right to read in the room where no one could bother them. That teacher knew that many of her students lived in housing where they shared a small space with several other people who did not always respect the students' desire for a quiet place to read and do homework. Many middle and high schools have experimented with the concept of a student lounge where students can earn the right to go and chill out when the world becomes overwhelming. Space and supervision are the two biggest problems, but schools that had students develop the plan had the most success. Students of all ages need time and a place to reduce their exposure to risk and to de-escalate following exposure. Principals' offices and counselors' offices are often used for this same purpose, but they do not meet the student criteria of safety and silence. While many students said they still come to school because it is safer than their homes or the streets, when they get to school there is really nowhere to go when they need a few minutes to regroup or compose themselves. Resilience requires the ability to de-escalate, evaluate, and prepare to meet peers and the requirements of the day.

Students must feel successful in some aspect of their lives to develop resilience. Success requires goal setting and achievement. Achievement of small goals, whether hourly, daily, or weekly, gives students a reason to return to school. One high-school freshman interviewed for this book was truant for all of his classes except technology. He was naturally talented with computers and felt that this might be his ticket out of a violent family situation. The computer teacher built rapport with him and started a weekly goal-setting session that included attending one other academic class per week. As the student became more successful, he eventually started attending all of his classes on a regular basis. Small successes made a big difference.

Werner and Smith (1992) longitudinally studied children from birth to age 32 on the island of Kauai, Hawaii. They found that schools can do many things to help children develop resilience, while further studies such as Winfield's (1994) cited the need for a developmental process that is reinforced constantly. Most researchers agree that the skills that can be taught to students to protect them from adversity include the following:

- reading skills. Werner and Smith (1992) found that fourth-grade reading skills are a predictor of successful adult adaptation. Children who can read can find alternate ways to solve problems.

- connecting with positive adults. All of us remember a teacher or other adult who had an impact on our lives. These mentors and role models usually show children how to solve problems and deal with adversity.

- goal-setting, decision-making, and problem-solving skills

- participation in hobbies and activities outside of school such as church groups, after-school clubs, sports programs, or service projects

- participation in school activities

- social skills and manners

- communication skills

- help-seeking behaviors

- task initiation and completion

- conflict resolution

What Teachers Can Do to Help Students Develop Resilience

Successful teachers who were observed and interviewed for this book shared the following ideas.

1 Teachers can make sure that they have current information about each of their students and recognize the impact that transition has on each student. One of the most accurate ways to gain information about students is to have a *reverse parent conference*. The teacher may hold this conference during regular conferences or issue a special invitation to parents. The parents are asked to tell the teacher about their child. The teacher listens and asks clarifying questions. When the parents are finished speaking, the teacher takes the most positive comments and builds on them to create a plan that will help the student succeed. Parents who are reluctant to speak can be asked, "Give me three words that describe your child." Those three words will give the teacher insights to help that child.

There are many phantom parents, parents who are never seen by the school. One elementary school did a parent census after the first set of parent conferences. Teachers were asked to list the names of students whose parents they had had no contact with so far that year. Using that list, administrator and teachers tried to contact the parents of those students in many different ways. While the list was not long, it coincidentally matched the list of those students who were failing in school and seemed to be least resilient. Every one of those students now has a mentor in school with whom they meet on a daily basis.

2. Teachers must develop an attitude in the classroom of focusing on student strengths rather than deficits. Teachers can have each student do a strength analysis at least once every marking period. A strength analysis simply asks students to list in a notebook at least five things at which they excel. Strengths do not have to be school related. They can relate to small tasks that young children do at home or jobs that adolescents do at home or for an employer. They can be character traits like kindness, respectfulness, or punctuality. Students may be skilled in spelling or math, or they may consistently get their work done on time. Resilient students recognize their own strengths; students who repeatedly say that they are not good at anything are candidates for intervention. Without a view of themselves as individuals with a future, students feel vulnerable. Strength analysis coupled with goal setting helps students to see themselves as persons who can withstand life's temporary risks.

3. Teachers can help their students have a vision of themselves in the future by teaching the goal-setting process. Teaching this process should begin in early elementary school and add skills at each grade level. It should be incorporated into the daily routine of elementary and middle school and used in a designated class in high school. Students who set goals become more resilient as they develop the belief that they are capable of having a degree of control over their environment, an internal locus of control that allows them to make choices regarding external influences. Goal setting is a protective and proactive process that helps students improve their ability to face high-risk factors such as bullies, gangs, abuse, drugs, and natural disasters.

One pregnant girl who floated for four hours on a piece of wood in flooded New Orleans said that she kept thinking of what her next goal would be as she waited to be rescued. She noted that her teacher had been teaching them to think of their futures and to set goals throughout the year, and she did not want to give up. When she was rescued, she asked to be put on a bus leaving the city so she could go to another school to graduate. Her goal was to finish school and make a better life for her child. She knew it was more likely to happen for her that year somewhere else. Her resilience was amazing in the face of horrific environmental conditions over which she had no control.

In elementary and middle schools, goal setting is usually divided into different types of goals, giving students many chances to learn the goal-setting process and find success. Here are some of those goal types:

- Daily class goals: Everyone in class will bring in their homework today.
- Daily individual goals: I will put my supplies away in their proper place.
- Kindness goals: I will say two nice things to other people in school today.
- Physical goals: I will eat a healthy lunch. I will exercise during break time.
- Skill goals: We will divide three problems using two-digit numbers.
- Community goals: I will help one other person today.

(See the entire goal-setting process on page 33.)

4 Teachers can offer a variety of ways in which students can communicate with them. Teachers have no idea which day will be the day students decide to trust and confide in them. Their conversation may be the only reason that children come to school or stay in school that day. There are several simple ways to provide ease of communication for students who may be shy or reluctant to speak in front of their peers.

- E-mail: Teachers can offer to answer questions, direct students to resources, or help them solve problems by e-mail.
- Notes: By placing blank note papers on the corner of their desk, teachers will encourage students to write them a note. They can ask students who have low resilience to write a note once a week just to let them know how they are doing in school. A box with a slot for the notes will ensure they remain private.
- Notification of schedule: Teachers can either post their schedule or tell students when they are available for help. High school students who need to connect with a teacher do not usually know all of their teachers' planning periods.

5 Teachers can emphasize historical examples of resilience in social studies, language arts, and science classes. Narratives and documentary movie clips provide teachers with opportunities to discuss the resilience that was necessary for historical figures to survive or accomplish a task or goal. Guided discussions about what it may have taken for these people to keep going after their initial failures help students recognize resilient behaviors.

6 Teachers can expect excellence in work but should show examples of what excellence looks like. Students must have the tools necessary to achieve excellence both in their homes and at school.

7 Teachers should know enough about their students to assign realistic homework. To complete tasks, students need both support and a quiet place to work, but many students do not have either of those elements in their home.

8 When using work groups in the classroom, teachers should assign tasks that can be successfully accomplished by all ability groups. After the initial success of all groups, teachers can assign more complex tasks. Students can work in groups of three initially; as the tasks become more complex and require more input, teachers can have each triad connect with another triad.

9 Teachers can develop a school-wide project that promotes cultural exchange and belonging. One high school planned and presented a cultural festival that promoted the music, art, sports, food, and literature of each cultural group that attended the school. The parents got involved, and the final festival allowed many students to use talents that would not have been recognized in a regular classroom. Several middle and high schools established community service projects that allowed students to connect with peers who normally would not accept them. Doing something for others is a good way for all children of all ages to build a sense of self-worth, which in turn builds resilience.

10 Teachers can show middle and high school students how to search for college and career programs. The end of class is a perfect time for students to research careers related to that class. Students with low resilience do not usually see themselves going to college and will not seek out counseling on their own. These students should be referred to counselors who can assess their options and encourage them to take advantage of the services provided by the school. Programs like the Princeton Review (www.princetonreview.com) offer information about colleges and universities, scholarships, and requirements.

11 In preschool and early elementary, teachers should work as teams over a three-year period to build strong relationships with students and their families. Teaming allows the teachers to promote growth in all areas of child development at this crucial time. Middle- and high-school teams can keep more students from falling through the cracks than can one teacher alone. Team meetings where teachers discuss all of the students on the team and how to support them (not just complain about them) are valuable for helping students with low resilience. Low-resilience students are not always academically at risk. However, they may be emotionally or socially less resilient than their peers, which will eventually affect their academic progress and, as a result, their desire to stay in school. The process is simple. During each team meeting, teachers talk briefly about ten students who have not been discussed before, documenting their assessment on a chart that has these headings: student name, status, commendation, recommendation, referral.

As each student's name is given, team members decide whether that student needs a commendation, a recommendation, or a referral to someone outside of the team. Even students who are not behavior problems or do not have academic problems may have little resilience and need recognition and support. This team-discussion form should not be used for assessing special education needs or solving long-term student problems. The goal is to recognize all students and to prevent avoidable problems.

12 Teachers should view students as at-promise rather than at-risk by providing opportunities for students to demonstrate their strengths rather than their weaknesses. Using alternate forms of assessment and alternate assignments helps students show that they know the material, not that they can take a test. If students are failing, teachers can ask them what they do know and how they can demonstrate what they know. For example, teachers can say, "Tell me something that you know about this topic that I didn't ask you." When teachers confer with students on their strengths, it allows students to build from them.

13 Teachers can work with parents of students of all ages to help them develop resilience in their children by not doing too much for them and modeling positive coping strategies.

14 Teachers can use questioning strategies that require critical thinking and dialogue.

15 Teachers can let students have input into the classroom rules or guidelines and consequences.

16 Teachers should use thematic, integrated curriculum whenever possible. Showing students connections among the content areas helps them find those connections independently and challenges them to look for those connections on their own.

17 Teachers can provide lessons on manners. Students build resilience by learning what to do rather than by being told what not to do. There are so many levels of civility and manners presented to students today that they usually do not know the norm for their culture or school. The content covered in classes like home economics, family living, life skills, and industrial arts is not always taught to all children. The examples that they watch on television are usually the antithesis of what is normally acceptable as good manners. During times of great stress in their lives, students need to know what to do rather than all the things not to do. This understanding is essential to students' survival.

18 Teachers should use role play to teach children appropriate ways to advocate for themselves. Students develop self-advocacy when the environment allows them access to teachers and the freedom to discuss

differences in a civil manner; they develop resiliency from advocating successfully for themselves. Teachers can show students models of how to approach someone they have a problem or conflict with and allow them to practice explaining their issue in a non-threatening way.

19 Teachers can show students how to use "I" messages when there is a conflict. "I" messages allow a person to state their feelings without confronting the other person. Because they do not put others on the defensive, these messages can lead to respectful conversation. For example, when students are angry at other students, they can learn to say, "I feel angry when you do that" instead of "You make me mad." They can say, "I don't understand that idea" rather than "Your idea is really dumb." Children of all ages can be taught to use the "I" message and need to practice using it when there is a conflict. Teachers employ this strategy as well.

20 Teachers can explain the basics of conflict resolution as a skill for developing resilience. (See pages 39–43 for sample activities.)

21 Teachers can provide students with practice discovering different points of view by using media statements, photos, or classroom incidents. For example, students can look for examples of resilience in news stories.

22 Teachers can survey all students at the beginning of the year to learn about them as people. Student surveys provide valuable information about students, such as their goals, dreams, fears, and strengths. A second survey in January will show how students may have changed. Teachers should look for traits to recognize in students and statements that might indicate risk. Survey questions should be open ended, as in these examples:

- What subject is easiest for you to learn?
- What do you need help with?
- Do you have a good friend in school?
- What are your goals for this semester?
- If you could change one thing about your school day, what would it be?

23 Teachers can start the school year with team building activities. These activities help students get acquainted with each other and the teacher.

24 Teachers can establish a program such as BUG (Bringing Up Grades) (Kiwanis.org) or On a Roll that recognizes effort for kids who bring up one grade per term without any others dropping. This can be done in individual classrooms and/or the entire school.

25 Teachers can spend a full day shadowing a student who may be defined as at risk by a colleague. Every three to five minutes, the teacher should document what the class is doing, what the student's teacher is doing, and what the student is doing. This snapshot of a day in the life of this student should be offered to the entire faculty without identifying the student. The teachers can brainstorm ways to help that student develop resilience. Administrators provide a substitute for the teacher who is doing the shadowing.

26 In the high school and middle school, teachers can establish a buddy program where each older student is responsible for one younger student. The buddy system should be in effect on the bus, in the hallways, and at school events. Teachers can celebrate the buddy concept.

27 Teachers can establish a "chill" section of the classroom where students can sit apart and do their work or diffuse their anxious feelings. One elementary school teacher has a rocking chair where students who are struggling can go and read by themselves for 15 minutes. In the middle school, teachers can designate a seat in the back of the classroom at a table where students can go to read, write, or just chill out. The concept is most successful when no one is allowed to engage with that student until the student gives the teacher a signal. The chill-out seat or section must have a time limit.

28 Teachers can implement the suggestions offered in Chapter 1 by the students. For both teachers and administrators who want to help students develop resilience, the old adage, "when in doubt, ask the students" may be the most effective strategy. For students with serious coping difficulties, counselors, school psychologists, and other health professionals should be consulted.

What Administrators Can Do to Help Students Develop Resilience

There are seven basic steps that an administrator can take to make sure children who are not resilient are being identified and that resilience is viewed by teachers as a necessary developmental skill.

1 Administrators must ensure that there is accurate information available to the teachers about every student in their classrooms. Teachers must be aware of special needs or circumstances that children bring to school, and that information should be updated every grading period. Teachers interviewed said, "If I had only known about the situation in the home, I would have adapted my assignments or changed my approach to the child." Schools must have a unified instrument that they can use to note lack of resilience in children and refer those children for additional help. Administrators can make teachers aware of the challenges that their students face at home by taking the staff on a bus-route ride during an in-service day before school starts. By seeing housing projects or homes without the basic necessities where students live, teachers will have a better understanding of their students' need for resilience.

2 Administrators can provide a time in the daily schedule when each student is recognized and spoken to by an adult. That person may be a classroom teacher, an advisor, or an administrator. The interaction may be informal or formal as in middle-school advisory or high-school seminar programs. The process that starts as "rug time" in most kindergartens, when the teachers talk to every child, needs to be adapted to an age-appropriate activity in middle and high school.

Every article on resilience identifies the need for connections between children and positive individuals in the school. Students who drop out of school stated that "no one really cared if I was there." One middle-school principal took that statement to heart and stood at the front door of his school every day and greeted every student by name as they came into the building. His cheery "Good morning. Glad to see you here today. Let us know if we can help you in any way" soon had an impact on students who learned that someone knew they were there and had offered to help them. It took forty busy minutes of the principal's morning, but he was adamant that nothing else be scheduled at that time. He wanted to be a consistent and significant connection for all the kids. His model and persistence paid off. Teachers began standing beside their doors to welcome students into the classroom, and students began to ask for help. Students who were posturing to quit trying began to think someone really cared. The whole school culture was turned around by the actions of a principal who understood that resilience demands connection.

Other administrators have assigned every student in the school to a mentor or advisor. Some buildings that house K–12 students established a buddy system so that every student has another student in the school to help them and watch out for them. Usually the students are two or more grade levels apart. The younger students find it reassuring to know someone who will answer their questions.

3 Administrators can establish a CARE (Concerned About Reaching Everyone) team in their building. A CARE team consists of an administrator, a teacher from each grade level, a counselor or social worker, a staff member (like a secretary, bus driver, or custodian), and five randomly selected students. This team meets monthly to discuss how the school is meeting the needs of all students. The focus is on efforts and activities that engage students. The purpose is to assess the student culture. If a problem is

identified involving a particular student or group of students, the CARE team designates someone close to the student or the group to try an intervention by sharing multiple ways of solving resilience problems with the student(s). The effectiveness of the CARE team was noted by one administrator who learned that a large group of fifth-grade students were bullying a small group of fourth-grade students on the playground. The CARE team found that the fourth graders were begging their teachers to stay inside during recess but would not say why. The bullying was subtle and usually included threats and some minor pushing or shoving. The playground supervisors had warned the older students to stay away from the fourth-graders, but the bullying group was too large to supervise. The CARE team members observed the playground themselves for a week and determined that the scope of the problem required a school policy on bullying as well as parent involvement to solve the problem. By having a formal CARE-team structure in place, the school alleviated a long-term and escalating problem for many students.

4 Administrators can assess the culture of the school and lead in the development of a curriculum that supports resilience. These are the steps for one popular culture assessment:

a. Place teachers in groups of six and give each group a large sheet of newsprint and markers.

b. Allow the groups fifteen minutes to draw a "typical" student. They are to include physical, social, intellectual, moral, and emotional characteristics in their drawing.

c. Ask teachers to list on the back of the sheet the students' current heroes, both in and out of school, and five values that students typically bring to school.

d. Invite each group to share its drawing and explain it to the other groups.

e. Using the information generated by the drawings, lead a discussion on what components the school needs to develop in a resilience-oriented curriculum.

5 Administrators can share with teachers the research relevant to their school culture. For example, at the early elementary level, screening programs designed to detect developmental delay or readiness may be a detriment because of the range in cognitive skills and abilities considered normal at this age. Students may be classified incorrectly, setting them on a course of high-risk schooling. Teachers who have norms for behavior that do not match the cultural norms of the students may label students in a way that puts them at risk with all future teachers. Screening programs must include a variety of screening instruments and input from parents, former teachers, and pediatricians (if possible).

A mismatch between the views of the students' home culture and those of the school system toward particular behaviors, such as help-seeking, puts students at risk. According to Nelson-LeGall and Jones (1991) most teachers foster an environment of independence where students must try to achieve on their own and seek help only after having failed. African-American child-rearing patterns promote help-seeking as a form of resilience. Children are encouraged to seek help in their community from an intergenerational network of extended family members, friends, and neighbors, but they find a value conflict in the classroom where the teacher insists that they "do it themselves." Administrators can share with teachers the research that supports the understanding of help-seeking as a resilience skill and give teachers guidance to change their own practices.

Middle-school administrators can remind teachers of the characteristics of young adolescents who are going through puberty. This stage of child development may require the most resilience from all children as it creates such drastic changes in their bodies, attitudes towards adults, relationships with peers and parents, and responses to school. Some administrators reported that they often place a "little-known fact about young adolescents" in the daily note to teachers and the newsletter to parents.

6. Administrators can support the teaching of goal setting by modeling and rewarding the process. One way to do this is to select randomly ten students and one teacher each Friday to have a snack with the principal and review progress towards goals. Everyone contributes to the discussion and the celebration reminds everyone of the importance of the process. As one principal said, "Goal setting in my building took on a life of its own as students asked each other and teachers about their goals."

7. Administrators can establish a crisis-intervention plan and make sure all teachers and students know what to do in a crisis. Students develop resilience when they have the necessary facts to handle stressful situations. Administrators can list on posters the first three steps students should take during a crisis so that students know their role. Schools should hold safety drills to give students confidence to handle stressful situations. In states and towns where threatening weather is commonplace, schools must involve parents and the community in the design of their plan. Administrators can schedule assemblies that teach safety practices for severe weather, school lockdown, bicycles and cars, the Internet, fire, swimming, and other types of situations relevant to the school's geographical location. Parents should be invited to the assemblies and be given materials so they can discuss the same issues at home. The assemblies ensure that students and families receive accurate information.

What Parents Can Do to
Help Students Develop Resilience

Children begin to develop resilience at birth. Even the most ideal families suffer from the top stressors for children and adults, including natural disasters, the death of a loved one, or a challenging move to a new town, neighborhood, or school. How adults respond to stress is the first lesson that children get in resilience. Many children seem to have the ability to bounce back from stressful situations and develop their own methods of coping. Those who study resilience in children (see References) agree that there are essential components to reducing childhood or adolescent stress.

1. Parents can foster a relationship with their children or encourage a relationship between their children and other adults. Every child needs a close relationship with at least one emotionally healthy adult in or outside of the family. That adult must help the child believe that he or she has everything necessary to be successful and overcome adversity. The adult must show the child that he or she is competent to handle life's situations.

2. Parents can help their children deal with emotions. When a child shows signs of fear, anger, sadness, or aggression, the adult should use words that describe that emotion and be empathetic. If the child does not return to his or her normal state, the adult should express confidence that the child can figure out a way to handle the emotion and offer to listen to his or her ideas and feelings.

3. The adult should restate children's ideas as they are offered and ask what they think might happen for each potential solution.

4. Parents can teach children how to deal with problems in a constructive manner. Parents can model problem solving by talking out loud about how they solve simple family problems and by identifying the steps they take to solve problems.

5. Parents can keep supplies on hand for self-expressive activities such as art, water play, clay sculpture, and drama.

6. Parents can teach children healthy ways to reduce stress. Exercising together not only reduces stress but also offers an opportunity for bonding between parents and children.

7. Parents can help children deal with change. It's important to give children plenty of time to prepare for upcoming changes in the family and to offer extra support for their feelings.

8 Parents can teach children how to ask for help and how to help others. As children become adolescents, they often seek support from their friends, coaches, teachers, family friends, or experts. Parents should make sure that those who are supporting their children are doing it in a positive way that builds the child's resilience.

9 Parents can praise their children honestly about specific achievements.

10 Parents need to help their children budget their time. They should not allow them to take on more than they can realistically handle.

11 Parents need to be able to differentiate between bad behavior and signs of stress in their children. They must recognize that children may act aggressively and take risks when they are trying to cope with stress in their lives.

12 Parents can teach their children how to make friends by modeling how to be a friend. They can talk to their children about what to do when they are rejected by someone they would like to be friends with.

13 Parents can teach a child how to help others through volunteer work or by completing tasks at home.

14 Parents can teach children how to maintain a daily routine. Learning an early morning routine is essential for most children.

15 Parents can monitor their children's environment. If a child seems unduly worried or stressed, the parent can determine the source and, if necessary, remove the source. For example, many children are frightened by the news, the Internet, or conversations that they hear only a part of.

16 Parents can teach children how to take care of their bodies.

17 Parents can teach goal setting one small goal at a time. They should focus on what has been accomplished rather than what has not been accomplished.

18 Parents can teach children how to manage their workload. For children who are easily overwhelmed and frustrated, it's a good idea to break homework and home projects into small doable parts so that the task is manageable.

19 Parents can teach their children to see humor in life and to laugh at themselves.

20 Parents can keep a scrapbook of the child's accomplishments to refer to when a crisis strikes.

21 Parents can help children see a stressful event in a broader perspective. Children have a difficult time understanding time and space, so adults must put those abstract concepts into perspective.

22 Parents can hold weekly family meetings to discuss how all family members are handling stressful events. They can discuss how change is a part of life. They can also share with children how they overcame stressful times when they were younger.

23 Parents should be able to recognize the signs of stressful behavior in all age groups and know (or find out) how to help children of different ages cope. For example, preschoolers may develop indigestion, be fearful of separation, and have night terrors. Elementary-school-age children may develop aggressive behavior, an inability to concentrate, sleep difficulties, or excessive clinginess. Parents should let the teacher know if their child is portraying stressful behavior and determine if the cause is from school.

24 Parents can stay involved in their children's school. They can read information from the school and volunteer to help whenever possible.

25 Parents can develop a parent network for parents of middle- and high-school students. This network is a listing of names of parents in the student's class who are willing to promise that there will be no unchaperoned parties, drugs, or alcohol available in their home. The parents on the list should be willing to be called by other parents when their children say they are going to spend the night or go after school to someone's house. This network protects those children who may have a hard time saying no to a peer, get caught in difficult situations, and do not have the coping skills to deal with the accompanying stress. (Bergmann, Brough, Shepard, 2009)

26 Parents can use the seven C's of resilience by Dr. Ginsburg (2006), mentioned earlier in this chapter, to help children develop their abilities, coping skills, and inner strengths.

27 Parents can contact specialists when necessary. If children do not respond to efforts to build or instill resilience, parents can seek professional help from the school counselor or a pediatrician. Parents should not assume that the child's sadness, anger, or frustration will go away by itself.

28 Parents can give children boundaries. Kids need something to bounce against when facing adversity. They need to understand that there are limits in the world that help people live together in harmony.

29 Parents can encourage their children to participate in extracurricular activities. Organizations often teach resilience through the goal-setting process. For example, after school clubs, church programs, and sports teams all help students feel successful. Children who do not participate in any outside activities may not get the reinforcement that they need to become resilient.

Summary

Researchers agree that children need support to develop resilience. A partnership between the parent, school, and community is essential for the development of resilient children. Youngsters need to feel socially competent and autonomous and have high expectations for success, with the support necessary to achieve it, and also have opportunities for participation and responsibility. Some students seem to have an endless supply of resilience. They overcome physical handicaps, parental abuse, or constant moving to new places and still manage to succeed and grow. Resilience can be modeled and taught. It may be the most necessary of life skills.

Teachers and administrators can implement a variety of strategies in the school to foster the development of resilience. Perhaps the best exercise that teachers and administrators can do is to have conversations with students whom they perceive to have developed a great deal of resilience and ask them how they became so successful.

References and Resources

American Academy of Pediatrics. *Giving your child roots and wings.* Center for Applied Research and Educational Improvement (CAREI) <www.cehd.umn.edu>

American Psychological Association (2007). *10 Tips for building resilience in children and teens.* Resilience Guide for Parents and Teachers.

Benard, B. (1991). *Fostering resiliency in kids: Protective factors in the family, school and community.* San Francisco, CA: Far West Laboratory for Educational Research and Development.

Bergmann, S., Brough, J. and Shepard, D. (2008). *Teach my kid I dare you.* Larchmont, New York: Eye On Education.

Brough, J., and Bergmann, S., (2006). *Teach me I dare you!* Larchmont, New York: Eye On Education.

Building resiliency in children, Handout #29. Child Action, Inc. Sacramento, CA. 95827 <www.childaction.org>

Center for Research on the Education of Students Placed At Risk (CRESPAR) <www.csos.jhu.edu/crespar>

Children, Youth and Families Education and Research Network (CYFERnet) <www.cyfernet.org>

Ginsburg, K. (2006). *A parent's guide to building resilience in children and teens.* Elk Grove Village, IL: American Academy of Pediatrics.

Goldstein, S. (March 2009). *Building resilience in children with challenges,* speech summary by NCLD staff. Retrieved from <www.ncld.org/ld-basics/keys-for-success/self-development/building-resilience-in-children>

Krovetz, M. (1999). *Fostering resilience: Expecting all students to use their minds and hearts well.* Thousand Oaks, CA: Corwin Press, Inc.

McClain, B. (Winter, 2007). *Healthy Children Magazine.*

National Child Traumatic Stress Network (NCTSN). <www.nctsnet.org>

National Institute on Drug Abuse/National Institutes on Health (NIDA/NIH). <www.nida.nih.gov>

Nelson-LeGall, S., and Jones, E. (1991). Classroom help-seeking behaviors of African American children. *Education and Urban Society,* 24 (1), 27–40.

Raising Resilient Children Foundation. <www.raisingresilientkids.com>

Rutter, M. (1987). Psychosocial resilience and protective mechanisms. In J. Rof, A. Masters, D. Chichetti, K. Nuechterlain, and S. Weintraub (Eds.) *Risk and protective factors in the development of psychopathology* (pp. 181–214). New York: Cambridge University Press.

Saewyw, E., Wang, N., Chittenden, M,. Murphey, A., and the McCreary Center Society (2006). *Building resilience in vulnerable youth.* Vancouver, B.C.: The McCreary Center Society.

Taylor, A.R. (1991). Social competence and the early school transition: Risk and protective factors for African American children. *Education and Urban Society,* 24 (1), 15–26.

Werner, E .E, and Smith, R. (1992). *Overcoming the odds: High risk children from birth to adulthood.* Ithaca, NY: Cornell University Press.

Winfield, L. (1994). *Developing resilience in urban youth.* Urban Monograph Series. Oak Brook, IL: North Central Regional Educational Laboratory.

Strategies, Lessons, and Activities for Teaching
RESILIENCE

Goal Setting

Teach goal setting through the following five steps.

Step 1: Goal Language and Initial Steps

Elementary school students should be introduced to the goal-setting process by asking them what makes them feel good in school. Responses usually include the areas of peer relations, organizational tasks, content mastery, or interaction with adults. They can also be introduced to goal setting in other areas of their lives. Parents can be taught to use the language of goal setting in their discussions about school experiences. A common vocabulary from the goal-setting process can be sent home and discussed during parent conferences.

Students who cannot or do not complete their work are usually not aware that if they set small goals, they will usually get the job done. One third-grade student saw every page in the math book as an impossible task. He quit trying to do any of the problems and was falling hopelessly behind. His teacher asked him why he would not do the work and he replied, "Many problems will take me all night because I don't understand all the steps." After a couple of catch-up sessions, the teacher asked the student to do only two problems to show that he understood. When he completed those two problems, he asked if he could do more. All he needed was to set and attain the goal to achieve a small part of the work in order to recognize that he was capable of more.

Many schools that have instituted goal-setting programs have set school-wide goals that are reinforced by the principal during morning announcements and through classroom visits and discussions.

Students can look for goals when they are reading articles and stories. Children as young as four can understand when someone is trying to achieve something and whether or not that person is successful. Television shows for preschoolers are based on the concept of problem solving and goal setting. Every episode of *Dora the Explorer* starts with a problem or wish, and then the characters consider several ways to meet the goal. Disney films are full of examples that children are familiar with. For older elementary-school students there are the infamous Superman and Superwoman, who always meet their goals. Children's literature can be introduced by having students look for the goal in the story and then determine how the character(s) met their goals. Older students can determine goal-setting strategies used by literary characters, historical figures, or scientists.

Step 2: Information Gathering

Information gathering is an important step in goal setting. When students are working on an individual goal, the teacher can ask them to list or talk about the information that they will need to reach that goal. Some goals are broader than others, but most require students to obtain some information.

For example, the simple goal of putting supplies and materials in the right place requires that a person know where that place is located and when the supplies and materials are to be put away.

The goal of eating lunch requires that a person know where lunch is served, what is needed to get the lunch, and where to sit and eat it. The goal of completing math problems requires that a person know how to divide, multiple, add, and subtract.

While those may seem simplistic examples, they demonstrate the thinking part of the goal-setting process.

Step 3: Determining Priorities

Once students have gathered information related to the goal, they must determine how to use that information to meet their goal. Many times students get too much information and follow a tangent instead of focusing on the goal. Or they get discouraged with information overload and do nothing. While some elementary school students who go to the school media center to pick out a book may find the trip to be an adventure that offers many choices, others may be overwhelmed and not choose anything. To help students focus on their goals, teachers can have students write down three things they like to read about before they go to the media center.

Middle school students often have the same problem choosing a topic for their science fair project. Teachers should take time to list and discuss the topics students are most interested in to give the students an opportunity to set priorities for their project selection. Students should have a list of priorities for book selection. Learning to match the information to the goal is a skill that also helps in decision making. For example, high school students who are seeking college admission and financial aid information often get frustrated by the amount of paperwork required. They try to complete several goals at once instead of completing one and then moving on to the next. It takes a very resilient student with a strong support system to complete the college admission process or a job search.

Board of education members, administrators, teachers, and parents all have priorities that affect how they make decisions and accomplish goals. Focusing on and teaching how to set priorities is essential. A board of education that does not work with a strategic plan based on a community-selected set of goals and priorities will find itself in a political quagmire when the budget is developed. An administrator who has a plan for the school's future based on a set of researched goals will make more progress than one who cannot articulate the goals and priorities of the school. Students are quick to recognize teachers who do not communicate the classroom goals to the students, set goals with the students, and establish the order in which the goals will be accomplished. Students describe those teachers as disorganized, disinterested, and uncaring.

The key is for teachers to take the time to have students gather information and then to require them to identify and write what information is most important to reaching their goal, what is second most important, and what is third. Once the students have selected that information, they can move to the next step, which is determining what action is necessary to reach their goal.

Step 4: Action Plans

Action planning is the part of goal setting where reality meets possibility. Students can be taught to set action plans for their goals by having them role play the process or discuss it in groups. Action plans are simple. Thinking about all of the possibilities is hard. Students will often set a goal that says, "I want to do better in reading." They then gather information on how they are currently doing in reading and what they need to do to improve. They learn that reading more is one solution. Their goal then becomes to read more. This is where the process changes to include assessment. Action plans usually include numbers that reflect how many tasks or how much time or money is necessary to achieve a goal.

Examples:

- ◆ Third-grade student: I am going to read two books that I have never read before during the next three weeks. I will talk about these books with my teacher and write six sentences about each book.

- ◆ Middle school student: I will go to the reading tutor every day for three weeks. I will ask for help with speed and vocabulary. I will do an assessment of my progress at the end of those three weeks.

- ◆ High school student: I will outline the chapters in my world history text and use those outlines to improve my test grades. I will share my outlines with my teacher to make sure I am highlighting the most important information. I will learn to outline correctly as a means of improving my reading.

- ◆ Teacher: We will identify all the children who we feel need the most assistance in our classrooms and what kinds of assistance they need, and we will share that information with each other. We will then identify the top ten children who are in danger of leaving school or failing and compile a list of ten ways we can help each of those children. They will be our priority for four weeks, and we will then determine if they have responded to the help.

- ◆ Administrator: I will adjust the schedule to give teachers planning time to work together to help at-risk students. This may require hiring substitutes for several half-days to allow teachers the necessary time to find resources for these students and to work with them.

- ◆ Board of education member: We will have a no-failure policy and give the schools the time and resources necessary to implement it.

Not having an action plan can lead to serious health problems for middle- and high-school students who embark on their own weight-loss programs. Without information gathering and priority setting under the watchful eye of a parent, teacher, or doctor, students often take harmful supplements or go on crash diets that affect their ability to learn. Many who are overweight choose skipping school as a means of coping with their weight problem. They are subjected to the media presentations of hundreds of products that are, at best, harmless and ineffective but can also cause harm to the developing body.

Step 5: Evaluation and Future Planning

With any goal-setting process by either individuals or organizations, the time will come when the progress towards the goal must be assessed. This is most effectively done in one-on-one conversations with students. One-on-ones are a means of having a regularly scheduled conference with a student that is short and purposeful. The function of the conference is for the student to update the teacher on progress or completion of a goal. It should be held in a part of the classroom where the student can have his or her back to the rest of the class. Some teachers are able to put two desks in the hall without disturbing another class. Most importantly, the teacher should be able to see the class, but the class should not be able to hear what is discussed.

Ask students to do some self-reflection in preparation for the conference. You will only need one or two prompts per conference, but the student should choose which he or she wishes to talk about. Remember that the purpose is for you to listen and to connect with each student privately. Teachers can give students the following prompts when the conferences begin, so that students have some time to think about what they might say.

1. My goal for this week is to _____

   _____ .

2. I (did what) _____ to meet that goal.

3. I think another good goal for me is to _____

   _____ .

4. If I could reach any goal, it would be to _____

   _____ .

5. The best thing that happened to me in school this week so far is that

   _____ .

6. The one thing I would change about my life in school is _____

   _____ .

7. The subject I like best is _____

   _____ .

8. The skill or assignment that I am having the most trouble with is

   _____ .

9. I want my teachers to know about _____

   _____ .

10. The easiest subject for me to learn is _____

    _____ .

11. My easiest subject is easy for me because _____

    _____ .

12. The best part of my school day is _____ because

    _____

    _____ .

13. The hardest thing for me to learn is _____ because

    _____

    _____ .

14. I wish our school had a class in _____ because I
    would like to learn about it.

15. I would like to be able to help others by _____

    _____ .

16. When I have a hard day, I just _____

    _____ .

17. I like to celebrate my birthday by _____

_____ .

18. My classmates _____

_____ .

If a student refuses to participate, have him or her write self-descriptions and hand them to you during one-on-one time. Remember that the purpose of this process is to connect with the student in a positive way. Some students need little time; others need a lifetime. If students appear to need more time, let them make an appointment to see you for a longer conference. Reserve judgment about what you hear, especially about friends, family, and colleagues.

The activities in this process were adapted from Decision Making Skills for Middle School Students by Bergmann and Rudman-NEA 1985.

For further lessons on goal setting, see *Goal Setting for Success* by Jerry Rottier and Kim Libby (NMSA 2005). This book and accompanying workbooks allow this process to extend over an entire year.

Conflict Resolution Strategies for Developing Resilience: Group Mural

Note: This activity is useful for third- through twelfth-graders.

Purpose: To build community by establishing baseline data about the similarities and differences of students in a classroom.

Time: 60 minutes

Supplies: One eight-foot roll of white paper to cover a wall in the classroom or hallway. There should be three columns on the paper: one column should have the heading "alike," one should have the heading "different," and one should have the heading "unique." Washable magic markers should be available for each student.

Procedures: Follow these steps.

Step 1: Divide students into groups of three. Have them list on a large sheet of paper all the ways in which animals, in general, are alike. Then have students list all the ways that animals, in general, are different. Have each group share their results with the entire class.

Step 2: Have them now list all the ways that they think students in their classroom or grade level are alike. Then have them list all the ways that they are different from each other and different from students in other grade levels. Invoke the "no put-down" rule. Be sure that students understand that you are talking about students in general and that no individual student's name should be mentioned.

Step 3: Each group should report their discussion findings to the entire class.

Step 4: Ask the groups to reconvene and answer the question:

How are members of our group unique?

Step 5: Ask groups to go to the mural and write their agreed-upon findings.

Step 6: Have students write responses individually to the following sentence stems:

From looking at the mural of our classroom, I learned that _____

_____.

From looking at the mural of our classroom, I wonder _____

_____

_____.

Brainstorming What It Means to Be Human

Step 1: Remind students of the rules of brainstorming:

> All ideas are accepted and recorded.
> People with ideas stand and present their ideas in turn.
> There is no ranking or valuing of ideas during the session.

Step 2: Place the following question on the overhead:

> Are there things that every single human being has in common?

Step 3: Have students brainstorm at least 7 minutes. Place all comments on the overhead or board.

Step 4: Ask the class to look at the list and decide whether each idea is something that everyone has in common, something that could be said for humans in general, or neither.

> *Note: For an individual to be human, every single one of the generalizations must be true.

Step 5: Divide students into groups of three and have them brainstorm what they believe humans must have to survive.

Step 6: Ask groups to share their lists with the class.

Step 7: Have each group brainstorm what each student in their grade needs to survive in school.

Step 8: Ask groups to share their lists with the class.

Step 9: Place students in new groups of six. Have each group of six generate at least 10 things they can do to help each other survive in school and in life.

Step 10: Have each group create a survival poster to remind students that they are all human and share the same needs.

What's in a Name?

Step 1: Place *What's in a Name?* for all students to see—either on the board, the overhead, or on a handout (see model on page 41). Then show the names (don't use names of kids in the class), one at a time. Ask students to write words that they think of when they see each name. It is quite likely that the names will elicit words about race and ethnicity as well as words related to age, gender, intelligence, weight, attractiveness, and trustworthiness.

Step 2: Ask students why they think this happens, and why it is natural for us to categorize and classify, but how it can lead to discrimination and unfair judgment.

Step 3: Ask students to read what they wrote about each name. List the descriptors next to the names. Ask the class to note any common words or descriptive phrases.

Step 4: Ask students what nicknames they are familiar with. Invite them to share some nicknames they have heard in the media. Discuss nicknames as a tool of acceptance or conflict.

Step 5: Ask students to write a five-sentence paragraph about whether they like their own name and why they like or dislike it.

Step 6: When they have finished writing, divide students into groups of five and have them read their paragraphs to each other.

Step 7: Have each group list five things they learned about names during this lesson. Have each group share their ideas with the entire class.

Step 8: Ask why knowing or not knowing someone's name can lead to conflict. Have each group brainstorm five positive ways to meet someone new or learn someone's name.

Step 9: Have each student complete the following sentence and turn it in:

As a result of today's lesson, I learned that _____

_____

_____.

Model for *What's in a Name?*

Susan Davis	Sandy Beach
Betty Lee Johnson	Mustafa Johnston
Rocky Rococo	Da'Jon Freeman
Carlos O'Malley	Maria Allendro
Songling Wu	Mohammed Abeel
Howdy Duty	

Conflict Resolution Lesson—The Sneetches

Purpose: To provide an opportunity for students to see how conflict often starts with name calling, bullying, put-downs, and stereotyping.

Step 1: Procure a copy of *The Sneetches* by Dr. Seuss and assign one page to each of 16 students.

Step 2: Ask the 16 students to take turns standing and reading their assigned page of the poem aloud to the class.

Step 3: Divide students into groups of three and ask the groups to list five ways in which humans can be like the Sneetches. Compile a class list.

Step 4: Have students complete the following sentence on a piece of paper to hand in or in their journals:

I will try to avoid sneetching because _____

_____

_____

_____

The Sneetches—written by Dr. Seuss in 1960—is now available as a book and a video and on YouTube. Additional lessons for teachers on this book are available at apples4theteacher.com.

Conflict Resolution Lesson: How Would We Adapt to a Different Environment or to Change in Our Lives?

Purpose: To develop the skills of resilience through adaptation in response to change.

Time: 2–3 class periods

Procedures: Follow the steps below.

Step 1: Depending on the age of the students, procure a large area where they can paint or draw comfortably in a large group. For elementary school students, the hall or gym floor works best. For middle and high school students, the paper can be placed around the room at a comfortable height for drawing. Use paper that is at least four feet high and six feet long for each group.

Step 2: Gather paints, markers, pencils, erasers, and floor covering

Step 3: Divide students into groups of four and assign a work area on the mural.

Step 4: Explain to students that they are going to change the classroom environment by creating a mural that will surround most of the room.

Step 5: Assign groups to find photos and articles about living under the sea. Students who live near a large fresh water lake may use that as their environment instead of the ocean.

Step 6: Have groups pencil in the drawings for their under-the-sea part of the mural.

Step 7: Assign one group to design living quarters under the sea and another to create food-gathering devices. The third group should design games and recreation and the fourth shopping areas.

Step 8: Discuss with students how they would have to change to live underwater. Ask questions like, "What would be easy about living there? What would be difficult? How would you have to adapt? What makes change harder for some than others? What knowledge would you need to gain?"

Step 9: Have students paint and color in their drawings.

Step 10: Place the mural around the classroom at eye level and give students an opportunity to celebrate their work.

Step 11: Ask students to discuss why changing environments creates conflict for humans. Have them brainstorm how they can make change easier on themselves and their peers.

Conflict Resolution Lesson: Conflict: It's Everywhere; It's Everywhere!

Purpose: To teach students how to identify different kinds of conflicts and how to resolve conflicts.

Step 1: Bring in a daily newspaper, an age-appropriate, approved movie, and/or a popular magazine for the age group you are teaching.

Step 2: Show several articles from the paper or magazine and then ask students to identify all of the conflicts they can find.

Step 3: Show the movie and have students identify the conflicts in the film.

Step 4: Ask them if the conflicts were resolved or are ongoing.

Step 5: Explain to students that there are three levels of response to conflict: easy, hard, and effective. For example, easy responses include leaving the conflict, denying it exists, giving in, and ignoring the situation. Hard responses to conflict include pushing, yelling, name calling, threatening, and breaking things. Effective responses to conflict include listening to the opponent, understanding, respecting other points of view, and resolving the conflict.

Step 6: Have the students choose a conflict in either an article or the movie and determine how the conflict was resolved. The teacher makes a list of the most frequently used means of conflict resolution in the media chosen.

Step 7: Ask students to talk about what they believe to be their own best way to resolve conflict.

Conflict Resolution: Case Study and Role Playing

Note: This activity targets third through twelfth graders. No student should be forced to participate.

Purpose: To help students learn to be resilient by practicing how they would handle a stressful situation.

Procedures: Follow the steps below.

Step 1: Divide the class into groups of six. Ask two volunteers to partici-pate in the role play. All others will be observers. Give the role players their role descriptions, but do not give the observers information about the roles.

Step 2: After the role play, ask each group of observers to suggest other ways the students may have handled the situation. After 5 minutes, let each group share their ideas with the class.

Role Play 1

Player 1: It is your first day to ride the bus to your new school and no one will move so you can sit down.

Player 2: You see the new kid who just moved into your apartment building get on the bus but he looks different from the rest of you. You see that he recognizes you and is heading for the seat beside you.

Role Play 2

Player 1: You are a bully who always picks the teams for kickball at recess and leaves some kids out who want to play.

Player 2: You stand on the sidelines at recess waiting to be chosen for a kickball team and then realize that you could start your own game and team in a different part of the playground. The class bully is not happy and comes towards you.

Role Play 3

Player 1: You forgot your homework and know you will get an F for the day without it. Your parents will be angry for you being forgetful. You know you have time to copy your friend's work if she will let you.

Player 2: You hear your friend say she forgot her homework again. You know she is going to ask you to copy yours, but you don't believe in cheating.

Role Play 4

Player 1: As one of your classmates comes up to you in the hall, you stash your drugs in your pocket.

Player 2: You see one of your classmates hiding drugs in his pocket as you approach him in the hall.

Role Play 5

Player 1: Your house was one of many in town damaged by a recent tornado. You feel uncomfortable wearing some of the clothes donated by people in town.

Player 2: You see a classmate wearing one of your old jackets and wonder how she got it. You do not remember throwing it away.

Role Play 6

Player 1: Your parents are both away in the military and you are living with your grandparents in a new town. You enter the cafeteria on your first day of school and see another student approaching you. This student is in a wheelchair.

Player 2: You see a student who is new to your school looking very lost. You wheel yourself towards him.

Resilience-Building Activity: Treasure Hunt

Purpose: If students are to feel a part of the school community, they must know and be known by their peers and their teachers. A simple way to get students acquainted with each other is to have them complete a treasure hunt in the classroom. The assumption in this activity is that we all have something to offer and that talent or skill or knowledge should be treasured. When students feel they have something to contribute, they become more resilient.

Procedures: Each student is asked to tell the teacher, in writing, two or three things that he or she knows or does well. Those items are then compiled into treasure hunt. Each student is given one copy of the items and asked to find at least one person in the room who meets that description. Students must sign next to their name on the treasure hunt.

See the example on the next page.

After all of the treasure sheets are signed, the teacher "corrects" the treasure hunt by asking the students who wrote the items to identify themselves. There may be more than one person for each criterion. The teacher should add one or two items to the treasure hunt. Ask students what they learned about each other by doing this activity.

Treasure Hunt

Name someone in this room who...

1. takes care of his or her own dog. _____

2. has a baseball card collection. _____

3. plays the piano. _____

4. knows all the multiplication facts. _____

5. can swim two lengths of a pool without stopping. _____

6. has lived in more than two states. _____

7. has lived in more than one country. _____

8. has written a story for others to read. _____

9. has two or more sisters. _____

Helping Students Develop
RESOURCEFULNESS

*"Most people think resources or the lack thereof hold them back.
In fact it is not lack of resources but rather lack of resourcefulness
that truly prevents people from achieving their dreams."*

Anthony Robbins

Resourcefulness on a
Deserted Island

Your entire class is on an island. It is three miles long and one mile wide. The highest elevation on the island is 300 feet at the north end. A cave is found within this hill that contains 500 pounds of wheat in an unmarked waterproof container. There is a fresh water spring on the island. The island is somewhere in a warm-water ocean. Thirty percent of the island is covered with vegetation. The island is not on any air or sea navigation chart. No plane or ship passes within sight of the island.

Whatever means you had for getting off this island is destroyed. No SOS or May Day call was sent. No one knows where you are or will come looking for you. Your physical condition on the island is exactly as it is at this moment. Your task is to determine, in exact order, the first ten things your group would do. You have 15 minutes and someone should take notes. Everyone in your group must contribute at least five ideas.

Participants need to use resourcefulness to solve this sample survival problem. It can be adapted to all age groups and is the type of activity that helps students develop problem-solving skills. Many current television shows are based on this kind of problem. Students see examples, both good and bad, of how resourceful people can become. The island activity provides a problem that is far removed from normal day-to-day problems of most students but requires the same set of skills. Students who have been allowed and encouraged to solve their own problems will offer ideas, listen to others, look for alternative solutions, and create new ways to solve the problem.

If students have never had to think for themselves, they might wait for others to solve this problem. It might be difficult for them to come up with realistic solutions. They usually try to avoid doing any thinking and tell the group leader that they would just stay on the island and do nothing. Because they are accustomed to others solving their problems, they do not see the necessity of doing the exercise, and some will not participate. (Adaptations of the problem are available on page 61 for elementary school students.)

A problem closer to home for many students involves gaining acceptance into a group at school. The resourcefulness necessary for solving this problem develops in most students, but those who have not had opportunities to solve problems for themselves may be in trouble. Students need to be resourceful on a daily basis in school. Consider this scenario:

> Mark is new to the middle school. He wants to make some new friends. One group of kids seems to be more popular than the others. Mark decides to try to join this group, and for three weeks he tries speaking to them. He even invites them to his home to play video games, but they refuse. He isn't being invited to join that group, either in or out of school. One day, he asks Tom, the obvious leader of the group, if he could hang out with them after school. Tom emphatically says, "No." Tom's group has requirements for being a part of it. Mark asks what he has to do to be a part of the group, and Tom tells him that he has to shoplift at least $100 worth of merchandise from a local discount store and not get caught. For over a week Mark ponders his dilemma instead of doing his homework.

There are many problems that get in the way of learning, and some of them create enough emotional and social stress that students may decide to quit school and focus on alternate ways of finding acceptance. Other problems that require resourcefulness include the following:

- being overweight and having to dress for gym class in front of peers
- being behind in one subject area because you do not understand the material and are afraid of the teacher
- not understanding what language is appropriate in school due to the lack of appropriate language at home
- being labeled ADHD, LD, BD, or one of the other "special" labels
- having a learning disability in one area but being gifted in another
- never being chosen for teams at recess or in gym class or in cooperative-learning groups

- being in trouble constantly because of the group you hang out with

- having no real purpose in life

- being caught in the middle between two conflicting adults

- not having economic security or a safe place to live

All of those problems require a set of skills that are found in resourceful adults. They are developmental skills that come from opportunities to practice problem solving, instruction in the problem-solving process, and models of resourcefulness.

What Does It Mean to Be a Resourceful Person?

According to researchers, a resourceful person is one who can make decisions, solve problems, think about his or her own thinking, and create new ideas or use old ideas in new ways. This person is also a positive decision maker who is usually a survivor in any given situation. This person typically has energy and a passion to succeed.

Because resourceful students are good problem solvers, they would find logical and creative ways to solve the island problem even if they have never been near an island. Resourceful students are evident every time one of them forgets homework or necessary supplies for school. Solving simple school problems of that nature is what develops resourceful adults. Resourceful students redo their homework before attending the class, even if it means getting marked tardy because they know that the consequences for being late are not as bad as the consequences for not turning work in on time. They have learned the system and how to make it work for them. One high-school freshman on the cusp of dropping out told interviewers that he knew that he had to come to school, but he had figured out that could he leave at 12:30 because teachers didn't take roll in the afternoon. Kids who are in danger of failing or leaving school can be resourceful in a negative way. They have learned to make their money on the street and see no need for an education. Their resourcefulness needs to be channeled by the school and significant adults in their lives if they are to succeed as adults.

Resourcefulness starts early when children learn how to go to school. They learn how to use creativity to solve a variety of social and intellectual problems. They learn to be accepted and play well with others. Resourcefulness is sometimes defined as common sense, but it is really the motivation to use common sense to figure things out independently. The skills necessary for resourcefulness include problem solving, self-reflection (thinking about your own thinking), decision making, and organization.

One third-grade student wanted to get new video equipment for the school because the equipment was always broken when the teacher tried to use it. He searched the Internet and found that he could save bottle caps for points and turn the points into new media equipment. He convinced the principal to let him ask other students to help. He presented his plan to the students and put collection boxes for the caps in each classroom. When the principal sent word of the project in the weekly newsletter, parents asked others in the community to help. Collection boxes were placed at bottle-return machines in all local grocery stores. A local business offered a pizza party for the classroom that collected the most caps. The third-grader went to the school board and explained his project. They offered to match whatever amount he made on the bottle-cap collection. Within three months, the school was able to turn in enough bottle caps to obtain four media players and two cameras—all because one third-grade student was resourceful enough to do something about the problem.

Teachers and adults model resourcefulness every day without realizing they are doing it. Teachers who encourage students to take on special projects and use creativity develop resourcefulness in students by modeling that behavior in their own daily work. On the other hand, those teachers who inspire resourcefulness may encounter adults in the work environment who still do not have the skills to be resourceful or do not believe it is important.

Consider the sixth-grade teacher who referred a record number of students (over 100) to the office during the first two weeks of school because the students did not have a pencil or paper. While his main goal was to teach responsibility, he disrupted his class most of the time, and the constant parade in the hallway began to disrupt other classes. Fortunately, this person was a member of a teaching team that believed in developmental skills and knew that sixth graders were developing organizational skills along with responsibility and resourcefulness. In fact, the students were so resourceful that they made a game out of not bringing supplies so they could get a break from the class.

The resourceful teachers held a team meeting at which they proposed a store for each classroom. Each student would contribute to this store one pencil and five sheets of paper, which would be placed on the shelf beside each teacher's desk. Students who did not have either a pencil or paper could borrow from the store, and instruction would go on without interruption. Students who borrowed were to replace the supplies at a later designated time. The teacher with the record number of referrals voiced his opposition, stating that he was trying to teach them responsibility. His teammates replied that he was merely setting up a system for the students to try to beat. One teacher asked, "At what age can we expect students to have the resourcefulness to be responsible?" Good question. However, the real goal of teaching students to be resourceful is not for disciplinary reasons, but because it is a life skill that will allow them to become fully functioning adult citizens who can solve problems and make decisions.

How Students Develop Resourcefulness

Students develop resourcefulness by being allowed actively to seek solutions to problems, by being given the time to figure things out independently, and by being given the freedom to act responsibly. Too many parents are impatient with the "I can do it myself" stage that starts at ages three or four, and they raise children who think they are incapable and incompetent. As children enter school, they develop resourcefulness in social, emotional, physical, moral, and intellectual situations. Those who have been encouraged to try tasks on their own at home have an easier time adapting to the multitude of tasks required in school. Teachers can usually tell which students are responsible for getting themselves ready for and to school and those who are not.

One seventh-grade male was responsible not only for getting himself to school, but also for getting his three younger siblings to the elementary school. He was highly organized, competent, and caring. Teachers had no doubt that he would have a successful future. Other boys in his class came to school without homework ("My mom forgot to put it in my backpack."), without gym supplies ("My mom didn't get it out of the dryer."), and without permission slips for field trips signed ("My parents forgot to sign it."). By taking over the responsibility for their children's actions, those parents inadvertently stifled their children's resourcefulness.

Children often develop resourcefulness when they are placed in difficult situations. Those situations require decision-making skills that are usually taught by default rather than as part of a plan. Consider the students in middle school every year who can choose to live with their noncustodial parent after their fourteenth birthday. Those students may be in a parental tug-of-war that affects them both in and out of school. If students have been taught, or modeled, an accurate decision-making process, they may have an easier time making their decision or use broader criteria. Those types of family decisions often affect these students' decision to stay in school and succeed or to drop out. Models of resourcefulness are essential to the development of this skill. Students who have resourceful parents or mentors are more likely to be successful than those who do not.

Many students want to be in school but are so far behind that they believe they cannot catch up. In addition, they may have poor reading skills that keep them from understanding increasingly difficult material.

Many young people have developed poor or no study skills and have no support at home to encourage them to try to do better. Instead of using problem-solving skills that produce positive results, they make excuses, blame others for their failure, and eventually drop out of school. Teachers who intervene and teach these students how to solve problems and make decisions can prevent students from failing.

Schools that are committed to developing resourcefulness hold invention conventions and encourage student involvement in future problem solving. There are daily examples of teachers and students working together to solve problems.

What Teachers Can Do to Help Students Develop Resourcefulness

1. Teachers can recognize resourcefulness as an essential life skill that must be modeled and taught to students.

2. Teachers can search content area materials for opportunities to teach problem solving and resourcefulness.

3. Teachers can provide alternative assessment opportunities for students to show that they have mastered the material (see sample on page 78).

4. Teachers can provide an independent-study project for students. The project can allow them really to explore something of high interest, design a way to show what they have learned, and receive credit for it (see sample on page 79).

5. Teachers can teach the decision-making and problem-solving process (see curriculum on page 62).

6. Teachers can allow students to keep a journal of their own problem-solving process.

7. Teachers can start a classroom project that helps other people and is planned by the students, recognizing that students may not be able to complete the project. Teachers should guide students through the process as the students plan, implement, and evaluate what they have done. Younger students will need lots of adult direction but should make the major decisions. For example, one classroom decided to adopt the vacant city lot next to the school and asked adult volunteers to help them clean it up. They learned that they also had to get permission from the city, purchase or borrow supplies, get something to put trash in, follow health laws regarding broken glass and other dangerous objects, and then figure out what use the lot could be to the school. This classroom project became a school project, then a neighborhood project, and finally a city project as the students raised the money to have a playground built on the lot. This resourceful fifth-grade classroom did what the city council had been unable to do for five years.

8 Teachers can involve students in future problem solving internationally. This type of international program is for fourth- through twelfth-grade students and has competitions at the regional, state, national, and international levels (www.fpspi.org). Teachers who do not wish to supervise competitions at those levels may offer a similar program in their own school.

9 Teachers can have students participate in developing classroom rules and guidelines as well as the consequences for each infraction. When students help establish discipline guidelines, they tend to own the consequences and understand why rules are made. If the rules are imposed, they become a source of negative resourcefulness for those students who try to beat the system.

10 Teachers can ask questions like "What if?" and "How could?" frequently in class. Simple sentence prompts for writing that require higher-level thinking skills, like analysis, application, and synthesis, force students out of the rote and into creative thought.

11 Teachers can have students design practice tests. These tests can be used for review and require students to organize, prioritize, and remember material that has been covered. Middle and high school students can also be encouraged to lead the class review before a test. Groups of students can work together to construct a study guide for a longer unit.

12 Teachers can design projects that involve experts, parents, and/or community members who have been resourceful. Students who interview veterans learn what it is like to be resourceful in the military. Those who interview or work with business owners learn what is necessary to run a business. Those who interview parents and grandparents may learn what is required to keep a family together during hard times.

13 As the school year comes to a close, teachers can have a panel of students from the next grade or level come into the classroom and answer questions about surviving the next grade. High school students can talk to middle school students, and middle school students can talk to elementary school students. Students should have a list of questions ahead of time, and teachers should remind them not to mention any names unless the names are a reference for help.

14 Teachers can encourage students to take summer enrichment programs that allow them to express their creativity.

15 Teachers can place a problem of the day on the board for students to solve when they come into the room. It could be a math problem, a language translation problem, a social issue, a school issue, or a personal-choice issue that the age group may be facing (such as college selection).

There are many books and sample problems at teacher sites online. The idea is to get students to think about problem solving every day.

16 Teachers can tour their students' neighborhoods to understand why students may or may not be resourceful.

17 When possible, teachers can use active, outdoor (or large group area) problem-solving activities that require students to be cooperative and creative. Some possibilities are Create a Game and The Witch and the Waterfall (see pages 72 and 73).

18 Teachers can use storytelling to promote creativity and resourcefulness. The teacher may tell the story, or older children can tell stories to younger children.

19 Teachers can assign students to make a video that promotes the ideas of accomplishment and problem solving. (See sample activity on page 74.)

20 Teachers can hold an invention convention where students can invent new gadgets for the home, school, or environment and display their inventions to the school and parents.

21 Teachers can show students an ordinary gadget (like a kitchen colander) and ask them what people 200 years from now might think it was used for if they unearthed it.

22 Once each week, teachers can use the last five minutes of a class period to have students complete the following sentences and hand them in.

- ◆ The most important decision I made today is _____

  _____.

- ◆ The most important decision I made this week is _____

  _____.

- ◆ The most important decision I made so far this year is _____

  _____.

- ◆ The most important decision I made so far in my lifetime is ____

  _____.

After three weeks, teachers can hand the students back their decisions and ask them to evaluate their own decision making. Teachers should discuss the process of decision making and continue asking those questions for the rest of the school year.

23 Teachers can provide an opportunity for students to choose a service project by having an agency fair. They can contact local service agencies and ask them to come for one hour to explain their programs and needs to students. Teachers can put all of the agencies in the gym or cafeteria so students can "shop" for the one they wish to adopt for the year. After the fair, students can hold a class meeting to discuss and choose a project for the year. If students wish to participate in the agency search, they could represent a cause (such as helping the Haitian earthquake victims) by preparing the necessary information for their peers and acting as an agency representative. In many schools, the student councils set up the agency fair.

24 Teachers can use student-led conferences as a means of teaching students to be organized, articulate, and self-evaluative. The skills students need to plan and maintain a conference for parents are essential skills for resourcefulness.

25 In the early grades, teachers can inform and encourage parents to allow students to try to do things themselves before stepping in and doing it for them.

26 Teachers can share with other teachers ideas that have worked for them in helping students develop resourcefulness or creativity by designing a school Web site for teacher sharing.

What Administrators Can Do to Help Students Develop Resourcefulness

1 Administrators can model and support teachers' efforts to teach problem solving by allowing time and providing materials and training. They can creatively schedule time each week for special projects, assemblies, or creative classes. One school district offers one hour per week for creative school-wide projects and community service, while another offers one day per month when problem solving and the arts are featured for students and teachers in workshops taught by parents and community volunteers. Students learn everything from ethnic cooking to robotics.

2 Administrators can provide information to teachers and parents about problem-solving competitions in which they can involve their students. Odyssey of the Mind, robotics, writing competitions, future problem solvers, and math competitions can be held annually.

3 Administrators can create a student advisory board to the administration and ask the students to help solve school problems that directly

affect them. For example, one school needed to cut back on extra-curricular activities because of budget shortfalls. Administrator speculated what might be cut, but when a group of students was asked to give their input, they noted that the school had far too many of the wrong types of activities. No one had asked the students what they wanted to do. Activities in place because of tradition were replaced by fewer activities that drew more students. Many schools have student juries that assist students with peer-to-peer difficulties and in school problems.

4 Administrators can offer a decision-making class as a part of the curriculum at the middle- and high-school levels. At the elementary-school level, administrators can provide in-class materials for teachers on decision making and problem solving (see activities on pp. 61–76).

5 Administrators can connect with a local recreation area for an outdoor-education, group problem-solving experience for students. These experiences provide an opportunity for students to show their skills and resourcefulness.

6 Administrators can invite successful business and industry professionals and artists in the community to come and talk to students about resourcefulness. They can discuss how they became successful in their fields and what skills the students need to develop.

7 Administrators can work with their staff to develop a school-wide or system-wide unit on problem solving. A committee can explore each content area for examples of problem solving that can be used to support the general teaching of the problem-solving process. By implementing the curriculum over an entire semester, students would have numerous opportunities to use the process and evaluate their skills. For example, language arts classes could explore what problem(s) the story characters face. Science classes could choose a scientific problem at each grade level for student projects. Physical education classes could work on health issues. Social studies classes could focus on how our ancestors solved problems or on how to develop citizenship skills. By the end of the semester, students should be able to recognize the steps that they or other problem solvers use.

8 Administrators can create a parent advisory council that provides the school with input on issues from a parental point of view. Using the resources in the parent community will help the school.

9 Because not as many parents get involved in the middle and high school as they do in the elementary school, administrators can establish a system for parents to volunteer in nontraditional ways (Bergmann, Brough, Shepard, 2008).

10   Administrators can network with community groups who can provide opportunities for students to solve problems and use their creativity. Many elementary schools sponsor annual school fairs that involve various community groups and engage their support. Safety programs are available from many state police offices or local fire departments. Dentists and doctors often provide evening programs on health issues. If each classroom is responsible for finding one community volunteer for a school event, the students will develop resourcefulness.

11   Administrators can support programs in their school that provide opportunities for children to develop their artistic ability, dramatic flair, or technological wizardry. If the system does not provide opportunities for creativity, students may develop negative resourcefulness as they express their creativity by looking for ways to beat the system.

12   Administrators can hold a teacher-exchange day for teachers who wish to try teaching another grade level or another subject area. Teachers can put their names in to be drawn for a determined day in the future. Only those who agree to the exchange program may be in the drawing. Once the names have been drawn, each teacher meets with the teacher they will replace to share essentials like students' names, lesson plans, and schedules. Many administrators try to make the exchange day on April 1.

13   Administrators can provide parents and teachers with a student information sheet that allows them to share their view of the child's strengths and needs (see sample on page 77).

What Parents Can Do to
Help Students Develop Resourcefulness

1   Parents can let kids try to do things for themselves and keep trying until they conquer the task. The famous "I can do it myself" stage of three- and four-year-olds represents their personal insistence to be resourceful. Unless the activity is unsafe, it is best for parents to let them try. For example, parents can find opportunities to inspire confidence and motivation in their children by allowing them to dress themselves, brush their teeth, fasten zippers, tie shoes, and clean their rooms. If parents continually do these tasks, their children will continue to be dependent into the teenage years.

2   Parents can resist robbing their children of chances to succeed in order to avoid their own inconvenience. If the children need to do something and cannot find their equipment, it's important to let them search for it or solve the problem in another way. If they are late because they cannot find the lost item, they can deal with the consequences. If teenagers

have not completed an assignment, parents can guide them by offering to review the assignment with them instead of doing it for them. If parents want children to be resourceful, they should not rush them to make decisions. Thinking through the decision-making process takes time. Parents should not do things for their kids just to save time.

3. Parents can let kids initiate and design their own creative activities from dress up to drama to sandlot baseball to starting their own business, whether it is a lemonade stand or a lawn service. Parents may serve as consultants but should not do the work.

4. Parents can give their children the facts about drugs, alcohol, sex, and Internet use and tell them how they feel about these issues and why. Children will make decisions about these topics that parents may not know about, so parents should give them information to help them do so and answer all of their questions.

5. Parents can teach their children to communicate with adults and advocate for themselves by giving them examples of what to say in certain situations and teaching them manners instead of speaking for them. Parents can also teach them how to compliment and how to apologize.

6. Parents can recognize that resourceful children are not passive. They do not use television or video games to fill their time. They learn passion for doing things by participating in activities. A family discussion about how much television and video time is reasonable and how it should be used will help children set their own limits, stick to them, and think about alternatives.

7. Parents can hold family meetings on a weekly basis to discuss other family issues as well and to allow everyone to express their points of view. While they may not make the final decision, children will learn resourcefulness by participating in the discussion and having input into major family decisions such as vacation choices, purchases, and family events.

8. Parents can organize household schedules and responsibilities so that their children have at least one chore.

9. Parents can share their own stories about growing up and their failures and successes.

10. Parents can teach their children the decision-making process.

11. Parents can help their children set goals.

12 Parents can understand what is expected of their children in school and communicate regularly with their teachers.

13 Parents can make sure that their children have a library card and use it.

14 Parents can pose thoughtful questions to their children so that they have to think about the answer. For example, they can ask "What if" questions and take the time to listen to their responses.

15 Parents can recognize that resourcefulness develops when children fail at a task and learn another way of doing it. When children try but fail, parents have an opportunity to encourage them to try again and again.

16 Parents can celebrate success when their children are resourceful.

Summary

Children develop resourcefulness by being active, independent decision makers who are involved in their family, their school, and their community. Resourceful children are able to see issues from many sides, resolve conflicts, and create new ideas. They are not passive or dependent on their parents, teachers, or peers. Resourcefulness is a skill that people develop very early in childhood. It is observable in classrooms, on sports teams, and in the home. It requires that children understand that there is a process for decision making and problem solving and that using that process will help them make better decisions. Resourceful children are fact finders and need support as they learn to move from the known to the unknown. They are risk takers who know where and how to get support for their ideas. They can be both negative and positive in their efforts. Parents and teachers play an integral role in the development of resourcefulness when they allow the children to try, fail, and try again.

References and Resources

Bergmann, S., Brough, J. and Shepard, D. (2008). *Teach my kid I dare you*. Larchmont, New York. Eye On Education.

Bergmann, S., and Rudman, G. (1985). *Decision-making skills for middle school students*. Washington, DC: National Education Association.

Cushman, K. (2003). *Fires in the bathroom: Advice for teachers from high school students*. New York: The New Press.

Future Problem Solving Program International, Inc. <www.fpspi.org>

Gurian, M. (1996). *The Wonder of boys*. New York: G.P. Putnam.

Gurian, M. (2002). *The wonder of girls. Understanding the hidden nature of our daughters*. New York: Atria Books.

Gurian, M. and Henley, P. (2002). *Boys and girls learn differently*. San Francisco, CA: Jossey-Bass.

Project Adventure, Inc., P.O. Box 100, Hamilton, MA 01936 <www.pa.org>

Smart, B. and Mursau, K. (2006). *Smart parenting: How to raise happy, can-do kids*. <www.asksmartparenting.com>

Tate, M. (2003). *Worksheets don't grow dendrites*. Thousand Oaks, CA: Corwin Press.

<www.wilderdom.com/games/descriptions/SurvivalScenarios.html> (a great resource for activities such as the Island Activity described on page 61)

Positive Learning Systems <www.characterlinks.com> (Offers sample lesson plans on building resourceful students)

Strategies, Lessons, and Activities for Teaching
RESOURCEFULNESS

Island Activity

Note: This activity is for elementary students. Use the activity on page 47 for middle or high school students and adults. The process is the same for all age groups.

Step 1: Hand out a copy of the island scenario to older elementary school students. Read it aloud to groups of five or six students.

You are all on an island. You have been shipwrecked there and cannot get off the island by yourselves. It is three miles long and one mile wide. It has one big hill that has a cave in it. The cave has a container of wheat that is still good. Near the cave is a fresh water spring and a small river. The island is in a warm water ocean and has many trees and plants. There are a few iguanas, some squirrels, and many birds. There are no people except yourselves, and there are no shelters. There is certainly no cell phone service, no television, *and no* computers. It may be a long time until someone finds you, so you need to decide what you will do.

Step 2: Say to students, "Your job is to decide, in exact order, the first 10 things you will do. Everyone in the group should make a suggestion, and then the group should decide on your top ten ideas. You have 15 minutes to make your decision."

Step 3: When the 15 minutes are up, ask each group to share their top 10 by writing them on the board. The lists will not be the same, and there is really no correct answer. In activities such as this one, the goal is the process, not the content. Then have the class identify the similarities and differences among the lists by circling the similarities on the board and underlining the differences.

Step 4: Ask students to go back to their original groups and answer the following questions on paper.

1. Why did your group select your first thing to do? Did everyone agree that this was the most important?

2. What questions did you have as you selected your top 10 items?

3. How did your group decide on the order of the items?

4. What did you need to know to solve this problem?

5. Was your goal to survive on the island or to try to get off of the island?

6. What skills did you need to select your top 10?

7. Why is practicing this type of activity important to your future?

Step 5: Have the groups share their answers with the class. Summarize the activity for the students.

Step 6: For additional practice, have each student write a problem similar to the island scenario that they have been involved in, read about, or seen in the media. Have them use the island activity as a model.

Step 7: Select one or two of the students' problems and have the class complete the process again.

The Decision-Making Process—an Introduction

Note: This process can be taught to children starting at the fourth-grade level. While younger children understand the concept of decision making, they usually do not have enough decisions to make on their own to make the process important to them.

Starting at about fourth grade, students are faced with ever-increasing pressures to make decisions for themselves both in their daily lives and as they plan for their futures. They are bombarded with information, possibilities, family pressures, school expectations, and societal stressors. Most students do not realize that they make at least twenty routine decisions a day—from deciding to get up and go to school to using their time to study, do hobbies, watch television, play video games, engage in recreation, eat, and sleep. Children do not believe that any conscious thought goes into decision making. Once they become aware that it is a conscious act and identify a process that can help them, they are surprised at how even the simplest decision involves their values and past history.

The Eight Step Decision-Making Process

Activity 1: Students make a written list of their decisions.

When asked to list the biggest decisions they feel they must make, early adolescents and adolescents have consistently listed the following decisions. (Bergmann and Vars Questions box study)

Note: Before reading the list to students, have them make a list of what they believe to be the ten biggest decisions they have to make each day, week, and year. As you read or post the list, have them compare their own list to the one below.

1. Who should my best friend be?
2. What should I do to find a best friend?
3. Should I always tell the truth?
4. Should I tell my parents the truth about what I think, feel, and do?
5. Should I do my homework?
6. Should I dress like everyone else or be myself?
7. Should I join a sports team even if I am not a very good player?
8. Should I try drugs, alcohol, and/or cigarettes?
9. Should I take risks?
10. Should I eat breakfast, lunch, or dinner if I feel that I am overweight?
11. Should I believe what I see on the news?
12. Should I do my best or just do enough to pass my classes?

Activity 2: How do people make decisions?

After reading the list to students, ask them if they have ever faced any of those same decisions. Ask them how they think most people make decisions. Each student should contribute one idea to the discussion.

Activity 3: The 8 Step Decision-Making Process

Share the 8 step decision-making process with students.

Step 1: Problem Finding: What exactly is the decision to be made?

Step 2: Problem defining: What are the basic elements of the decision, the who, what, where, why, how, and how does it feel?

Step 3: Information Gathering: What information do I need to make this decision in the parameters I have defined in steps 1 and 2?

Step 4: Information Prioritizing: What information is of most importance and what is of least importance?

Step 5: Values assessment: What do I believe in and how will my beliefs influence my decision? How do my beliefs compare with those of my family and friends?

Step 6: Alternatives and Consequences: What are the possible solutions to this decision? What are the consequences to me of each of the possible solutions? What risks are involved in each alternative and each consequence?

Step 7: Action: What will I actually do about this decision? When and where will I take action?

Step 8: Evaluation: How will I know if I made the right decision? Was my action appropriate for my beliefs, the information gathered, and the alternatives given? How did my decision affect my life?

Activity 4: Ask all students to write (anonymously) a few sentences about one big decision they have had to make. Then have them list the decisions they make every day.

Activity 5: Ask students to evaluate one of their decisions and see how many of the 8 steps they used in making the decision.

Activity 6: Have each student share one or two comments about their decision making.

Activity 7: Use at least two examples appropriate to the age group from the list below and have students use the 8 steps to make the decision:

Elementary School Students

Option 1: During recess on Tuesdays and Thursdays, everyone goes outside to play dodge ball or kickball. You love to play, but you also love to read sports stories. Your teacher says that next Tuesday, students can opt to stay inside and read quietly instead of going out to play dodge ball. You have to sign up for one or the other today. Which will you choose?

Option 2: Your parents have finally given in and told you that you can get one pet. You must be able to take care of it all by yourself. You live in a small house with a small yard on a busy street. What type of pet will you choose?

Option 3: You have finally saved enough money to get a game system. Which one will you buy?

Middle School Students

Option 1: You want to get a part-time job in the summer to save money for a new bike. How do you go about finding a job?

Option 2: You want to help the people of Haiti and have some good ideas, but you do not know whom to approach to help you. How will you solve this problem?

Option 3: You are getting a B in social studies and could get an A if you do a spectacular project this term. What will you do?

High School Students

Option 1: Your parents want you to go to college, but you think you want to be a chef. You would like to work as a chef for a year to see if you really like it. You have very good grades and could go just about anywhere. What will you decide to do?

Option 2: You have a friend who is an outstanding athlete, but lately, she has been drinking excessively on the weekends. She is missing school on Mondays and then missing practice. She tells you she needs help. What do you do?

Option 3: You have just entered the ninth grade in high school and are being bullied and hazed by upper classmen in the locker room before gym class. If you don't check in and out of the locker room, your grade goes down each day. What will you do?

Activity 8: When students have finished working one of the decisions through the 8 steps, pair students with a partner to discuss their work.

Activity 9: Have each set of partners write two questions they have about decision making and share those questions with the class.

Activity 10: Assign students to log the decisions that they make over an entire weekend and bring the list to the next class. (See decision-making log on page 69.)

Activity 11: Students present their lists of decisions made over the weekend and a class list is compiled on newsprint or a transparency for future reference.

Activity 12: Ask students to rank order the five most important decisions from their own lists and from the class list and give their reasons. Discuss the difference between a critical and non-critical decision.

Information Gathering and Prioritizing

Purpose: A critical part of the decision-making process is information gathering and prioritizing. This skill is also crucial to the development of resourcefulness. Most students will admit that they do not formally gather information when making decisions. They usually do whatever "feels good" or "seems right" at the time. This process can be practiced in any content area and is actually taught in many subjects.

Procedures: Place the following list on the board or on an overhead projector.

Information-Gathering Steps

1. Determine what information is needed.
2. Determine accurate sources of information.
3. Gather information.
4. Prioritize information from most useful to least useful.
5. Eliminate information that is not useful.
6. Incorporate information into decision.
7. Store information for future decisions.

Activity 1: Divide students into groups of four or five and give them one of the following decisions to make.

Decision 1: Sally is planning her birthday party but she does not have many friends. There is a very popular group of kids at school, but she does not know them. She really wants to get to know them so she hands out personal invitations to each of them and invites them to her party. She does not invite the kids who have been nice to her as they were not her choice of friends. The day before her party, the students that she did invite all call and say that they will not come to her party. Her parents have planned a big party and are eager to meet Sally's friends. If you were Sally, what would you do?

Decision 2: Your classroom must build a booth for the school mall in the hall and come up with a product to sell in that booth. What product will you sell?

Decision 3: Your principal comes to your class and tells you that they are going to change the school lunch menu. They want to offer healthier foods that students will eat. Each class is being asked to suggest three new menu items. Those items will be placed on a ballot with the items from other classes, and all the students will vote. What three items should your class recommend?

Decision 4: Your school band has been invited to play at Walt Disney World in Florida over spring break. You are the only tuba player and you have never been to Disney World. Your entire family already has airline tickets to see your grandparents in California. You have not seen them in two years, and your grandfather is very ill. What would you decide to do?

Decision 5: You are on your way home from school and you witness an accident. There appear to be people injured. What would you do?

Give each group the following list of questions:

1. What is the decision to make?
2. What information do you need to make the decision?
3. What information is critical, and what is not?
4. How will you gather information?
5. Can the decision be made based on the information that you have?
6. If you make a decision, what will it be?

Ask groups to share their answers with the class.

Then have students role play the decision and their process.

Decision-Making Alternative Action Search

Step 1: Divide students into groups of four or five.

Step 2: Using the five scenarios on page 66, the decisions listed for information-tion gathering, have each group select one of the scenarios.

Step 3: Explain that the alternative-action process is a brainstorming and matching exercise that we go through mentally when we solve problems and make decisions. It is the "What if" component of decision making.

Step 4: Allow at least three minutes for each group to brainstorm all of the ways they can think of to solve this problem. Assign one person in each group to write all of the suggestions on a piece of paper.

Step 5: Once the group is done brainstorming, have them consider "What would probably happen if I did this?" for each suggestion.

For example, in the scenario about Sally's birthday party, students might write "Sally could call all the people she did not originally invite and invite them. What would probably happen if she did this? They would not attend the party because they know they were her second choice."

Or, they might write "Sally could tell her parents the truth and hope they would celebrate her birthday with her."

In the School Band to Disney decision, students may write "You go to see your grandparents and, before you leave, you teach someone else to play the tuba for the two songs your band will play at Disney. What would probably happen? The tuba would sound terrible, but you would not be there to hear it."

Step 6: After students have searched for alternatives, ask them to discuss why alternative action searches are essential to making major decisions.

Student Decision-Making Log

Step 1: Assign students to log the decisions that they make over an entire weekend and bring the list to the class the following Monday. (See the decision-making log that follows.)

Step 2: Have students present their lists of decisions made over the weekend and compile a class list on newsprint or a transparency for future reference.

Step 3: Ask students to rank the five most important decisions from their own lists and from the class list in order from most important to least important. Have students explain their reasons. Discuss the difference between a critical and noncritical decision.

Student Decision-Making Log

Students are to keep track of all the decisions they make in a weekend and fill in the columns on the log.

Decision	Alternatives Considered	Action	Result

As a result of this log, I learned that:

Personal Alternative-Action Activity

Procedures: Follow the steps below.

Step 1: Give each student a copy of the Personal Alternative Action Search on page 71 and have them complete it.

Step 2: Have a class discussion about why some decisions are easier than others. Ask questions like "What makes a decision critical?" and "How do your decisions affect other people?"

Step 3: Have students work in pairs and share the first situation from their Personal Alternative Action Search with their partner. Allow one minute for students to share their answers.

Step 4: Have each pair of students share the second situation with another pair. Allow one minute for students to share their answers.

Step 5: Have the two pairs of students share the third situation with another foursome. Allow three minutes for students to share their answers.

Step 6: Have the eight students in one group share the fourth situation with another group. Allow five minutes for groups to share their answers.

Step 7: Have the entire class share their responses to the fifth situation.

Step 8: Have students complete the following sentences. Collect their sentences.

As a result of this activity, I learned that _____

_____

_____

_____

_____

_____.

As a result of this activity, I will probably _____

_____

_____

_____

_____

_____.

Personal Alternative-Action Search

Directions: Read the five situations below, and answer the following questions about each situation:

- ◆ What would I do in this situation?
- ◆ How many alternative actions can I think of for each problem?
- ◆ What would be the consequence for each of my actions?

1. You forget to bring money for the field trip, and it is due today.

2. You borrow a DVD from a friend and lose it.

3. You are trying to finish your work in class, and the person next to you keeps talking to you.

4. Your family is moving to Chicago in April, and your mom says you can stay with your grandparents to finish out the school year.

5. Three students in your class are spreading lies about you on the Internet.

Group Decision Making and Problem Solving:
Watch Out for the Witch and the Waterfall

Purpose: To develop decision-making skills in individuals and groups.

Location: A hallway, gym, or other large space.

Supplies: At least eight carpet squares to serve as rocks in the river, and blindfolds for at least four people at a time.

Time: 20 minutes (15 minutes to complete and 5 minutes to process)

Step 1: Place the carpet squares two to three feet apart in a line across the room. They should be close enough together for students to step from one to another. Distance will depend on the age and size of the students.

Step 2: Divide students into groups of nine. Ask one student to be the wicked witch of the river. Blindfold four of the remaining eight students.

Step 3: Explain that the squares represent stones in a white-water section of a river at the very top of a waterfall. The group has been lost in the wilderness for a week and sees a cabin with smoke coming out of the chimney across the river. They know there is no help in any other direction. The goal is to get the entire team across the river without anyone falling over the waterfall. The four students on the team who are not blindfolded must lead the blindfolded students to safety. Once they begin crossing the room, the witch may steal any square that is not occupied.

Rules:

- The witch cannot steal a stone that is occupied.

- If any part of a your body (heel, foot, arm, etc.) falls off of the stone, you may not use that body part the next time you cross.

- Groups have 2 minutes to plan a strategy before starting to cross the river.

Step 4: Allow each group an opportunity to participate. Time each group crossing.

Step 5: When all groups are finished, lead a discussion that includes the following questions:

- What decisions did your group make before starting to cross the river?

- What decisions did you have to make after your group started crossing.

- What would you do differently if you were to do it over?

- What did you learn from this activity?

Resourceful Decision Making: Create a Game

Purpose: To help students make decisions as a part of a group.

Note: This activity requires a large area such as a gym, playground, or all-purpose room. If a large space and sports equipment are not available, this activity can be done using kitchen utensils that do not have sharp edges.

Procedures:

Step 1: Divide the class into groups of four (for small classes) or six (for large classes).

Step 2: Give each group three pieces of sports equipment (for example, a baseball, a cone, and a jump rope), a large piece of paper, and a washable marker. Do not give them three of the same piece of equipment.

Step 3: Set a time limit of 15 minutes.

Step 4: Explain the rules:

1. Each group must create a totally new game.

2. Each group must use all three pieces of equipment.

3. You cannot use the piece of equipment in the way for which it was originally designed. For example: You cannot jump a rope or throw a baseball.

4. Everyone in the group must participate in the game.

5. Every game must have three rules. Write the rules on the large piece of paper.

6. Every new game must have a name.

Step 5: Each group will teach their game to two other groups.

Step 6: On separate paper, each group will list the decisions they made during the design of their game.

Step 7: Each group will tell how they might do it differently next time.

Self Prediction Activity

Purpose: To get students thinking about the need to be resourceful.

Step 1: Ask students to answer the following questions on a piece of paper.

1. Where will you be 15 years from today?

2. What will the world be like?

3. Will you be married and have a family?

4. What will be the most important decision you have made during the past 15 years?

5. What will be the most important decision you will have to make in the following 15 years?

6. What will your occupation be in 15 years from now?

Step 2: Fold the paper, put it in an envelope, and seal it. Write on the envelope "Do not open for 15 years."

Step 3: Give the envelope to your parents for safe keeping.

Video Assignment for Developing Resourcefulness

Purpose: To write the script for and record a video that explains the problem-solving and decision-making processes to younger students.

Procedures

Step 1: Divide students into groups of three or four.

Step 2: Explain the purpose of the assignment and hand out sheets of paper for writing scripts and titles.

Step 3: Have groups complete a planning sheet like the one that follows, to help them decide what they would like to show in their video.

Step 4: Explain how to use the video cameras.

Step 5: Allow students to decide whether to make an in-school or out-of-school video.

Step 6: Provide students with class time to work on their videos.

Step 7: Schedule time for groups to share their videos with the class.

Video Planning

Names of group members: _____

_____

_____

_____

Script outline: _____

_____

_____

_____

_____

_____

_____

_____

_____

_____

_____

_____

_____

_____

_____

_____

Title of video: _____

Characters: _____

_____

_____

_____

Setting: _____

_____

_____

_____

_____

_____

_____

_____

_____

_____

_____

_____

_____

Plot: (How will you show the steps of the decision-making process?)

_____

_____

_____

_____

_____

_____

_____

_____

_____

_____

_____

_____

_____

_____

_____

_____

Student Information Sheet
(to be completed by parents)

Dear Parent:

   The staff at our school is very interested in helping your child succeed in school. We would like you to fill out this information sheet, which will be given to your child's classroom or homeroom teacher. The more information that you can give us about your child, his or her strengths or needs, and any concerns that you may have, the better we can plan the appropriate learning environment for each student. Thank you for your help.

Name of student: _____

Name of classroom or homeroom teacher: _____

1. Please identify your child's areas of strength.

2. Please identify any concerns you have about your child in school.

3. Please describe your child's learning patterns regarding organizational skills, homework style, etc.

4. In your opinion, what type of approach to instruction helps your child learn in the most effective manner?

5. Please describe your child's interests, hobbies, and skills that may not always be evident in the classroom.

6. Please tell us any family information that will help us to know and teach your child better.

7. What goals do you have for your child this year?

Alternative Assessments for Building Resourcefulness in Students

To show that I know the skills and concepts presented in this unit, I would like to

_____ create a video.

_____ build a model or diorama.

_____ create a song that tells the material.

_____ write a report with references.

_____ make a photo essay.

_____ put on a demonstration.

_____ design and paint a classroom mural.

_____ do charts and diagrams.

_____ interview community people.

_____ interview senior citizens and relatives.

_____ develop and teach a simulation.

_____ design and teach a game to the class.

_____ give a speech to the class or to younger children.

_____ teach the material to students who do not understand it.

_____ write a short story.

_____ write poetry about the material.

_____ design a game show using the material.

_____ develop an interactive computer presentation.

_____ set up an experiment.

_____ choreograph a dance for a small group to present.

_____ interview an expert on the topic.

_____ develop a project not listed above.

Brief description of what I intend to do:

_____

_____

_____

_____

_____

Signature of student _____ Date _____

Signature of teacher _____ Date _____

Independent Study Project

Purpose: The purpose of an independent study project is to allow students to explore an idea, concept, skill, or problem in depth. The topic of the project may be a part of a content area but can and should include topics that are interdisciplinary. Students complete the following contract and then hold a conference with the teacher and their parents for approval. The students are usually given an entire marking period to complete the project. Teachers teach organization and presentation skills as a part of the project. After all the students have completed their projects, they present them to parents and peers at a project fair. How the projects are graded and credit assigned will depend on the teacher(s).

In one school, students were provided with time once a week to work on their project. Students could do research on their topic, talk to experts, construct their models, or write their papers, stories, or plays. To discourage report-style writing and encourage creativity, teachers often suggested that students use the alternative assessments sheet on page 78. The key was to allow students to explore something of high interest.

Procedures: Teach students the process for doing projects:

1. State your topic, problem, or goal. State what you already know about it.

2. State why you are choosing this topic, problem, or goal.

3. List where you will get information and who you will use as experts.

4. Tell how you will achieve your goal. List at least three steps you will use.

5. If your project requires materials, where will you get the materials?

6. How will you organize your work? What will you do first, second, third, and so on?

7. How will you show what you have learned by doing this project?

8. How will you determine what grade you deserve on this project?

9. When will you start this project?

10. What help do you think you will need?

When teachers have completed the project overview and offered some examples of completed projects, students will complete the independent study proposal, have it signed, and hand it in to the teacher who will be mentoring this student through the project. Ideas for projects should come from the students first, but some examples of past independent study projects include the following:

1. career exploration for becoming a chef

2. design and building of a gas powered go-cart

3. a working model of the Hoover Dam

4. a play written for reenactment of the Gettysburg Battle

5. reports written with speeches given on sports issues, countries, and famous people.

Independent Study Proposal

Student Name: _____

Class: _____

Starting Date of Project: _____

Ending Date of Project: _____

1. The goal of my project is _____
    _____.

2. Why did you choose this project? _____
    _____.

3. Where will you get your information? (List five sources)
    a. _____
    b. _____
    c. _____
    d. _____
    e. _____

4. Whom will you ask for opinions or assistance? (List at least two people)
    a. _____
    b. _____

5. List three steps you will take to complete this project.
    a. _____
    b. _____
    c. _____

6. What materials will you use to complete this project? _____
    _____

    From where will you obtain those materials? _____
    _____

7. What will you do first to get started on this project? Make an outline of
    the steps you will take on the back of this form. Put dates by each step.

    _____

8. How will you show what you have learned from this project? _____
    _____

9. What help do you think you will need from the teacher? _____
    _____

10. With whom will you share your project? _____

Student signature _____
Teacher signature _____
Parent signature _____

RESOURCEFULNESS

Student-Parent-Teacher Conferences

Purpose: In this model, students prepare for the conference by keeping a representative sample portfolio of their work. Homebase or advisory teachers, classroom teachers in elementary school, or seminar teachers in high school can help students with their portfolios and teach them conferencing techniques. The goal is to help students develop communication skills regarding their work.

Procedures: Ask students to write answers to the following questions in preparation for the conference:

1. What have you been studying in each of your classes so far this year?
2. What are you most proud of?
3. What has been the hardest for you so far?
4. What did you do to deal with this?
5. What do you need to do to improve?
6. How can parents and teachers help you?
7. Describe yourself in the classroom.
8. What are your goals for the next quarter, trimester, etc.?
9. What might help you meet these goals?
10. Where might you get this help?

Conferences should take 15–20 minutes. Have student introduce and conduct the conferences. This is not the time for parents to have a conference with the teacher.

Helping Students Develop
RESPONSIBILITY

*"Few things help an individual more than to place responsibility
upon him and let him know that you trust him."*

Booker T. Washington

How often have teachers uttered the words "If only these students could learn to be responsible, they would be doing better in my class. They forget their work, they don't come prepared for tests, they don't seem to care if they succeed"? Not only are the teachers frustrated, but the students themselves often express dismay at their own behavior and inability to be responsible. Some even act irresponsibly on purpose to avoid doing their work.

Perhaps they have never had to be responsible for anything or anyone in their entire lives. Perhaps they are not trusted to do the right thing at home. Most likely they do not know what being responsible means. While many students get themselves up in the morning, fix their own breakfast, and get to school on time with completed homework, others fall further and further behind because of their lack of responsibility rather than their lack of intellectual capability.

What Is Responsibility?

Responsibility is a difficult characteristic to define as it also includes accountability, decision making, motivation, awareness, honesty, problem solving, resilience, resourcefulness, persistence, and emotional maturity.

Responsibility is a developmental skill that is learned from and usually regulated by adults until children can learn to regulate themselves. Responsibility and independence are related skills that develop throughout childhood, adolescence, young adulthood, and adulthood. Completing a task without teacher or parent supervision might be appropriate for a seven-year-old, but not a four-year-old.

Responsible children consider the effect their actions have on others and meet their own needs without interfering with others. They respect others and have confidence in their behavior. They know the right thing to do in most situations. Because responsibility is developmental, with varying levels of accomplishment within the same age group, parents and teachers are often concerned with the line between typical childhood behaviors and irresponsibility. For example, not all fourth-grade students have developed the ability to make good decisions or consider others when they act out and disturb the class.

Students may seem very irresponsible at school but be totally responsible at home. One parent was utterly amazed during parent night at her child's messy desk because that child always kept his room immaculate at home. At home, the responsibility of keeping a clean room meant time on the computer and television. At school it meant only that the child could not find things and was always late getting started with the lesson.

Responsibility can be defined as students' ability to control and manage their own lives by doing the following:

◆ planning for future events

◆ initiating and following through on activities

◆ asking for necessary help

◆ being on time

◆ taking care of bodily needs and hygiene

◆ taking care of belongings

◆ acting appropriately toward the environment

How Students Develop Responsibility

Parents have a major impact on the development of responsibility in children. If parents are either too controlling or too lax in discipline, children will not learn to take responsibility for their actions. If they allow freedom within clearly defined parameters, children will gradually learn to be responsible and have more success in school. Children who have been allowed to make choices and experience the results of those choices develop that skill and apply it to schooling.

Responsibility is learned by observing responsible behaviors. It is learned by watching parents, teachers, media personalities, leaders, and peers. When observation is combined with discussion about why behaviors are responsible or irresponsible, the child learns to differentiate and chooses to follow the behavior that appears to have the most positive outcomes.

Children learn responsibility by being involved in family chores and decisions.

They learn it at an early age when parents ask them to help with the dishes after a meal. That simple request is the one of the first times that children recognize that they can and should be responsible for helping. There are two types of responses that help or hinder the development of responsibility. The parent who says, "No thanks, we have a dishwasher for that task" takes away the opportunity for children to learn responsible behavior. The parent who gives children age-appropriate dishwashing tasks fosters the development of responsibility.

Children learn from understanding the vocabulary of responsibility when parents and teachers explain what they did, why they did it, what the consequences of their actions were, and how it made them feel. They learn when examples of responsible behavior are pointed out as they occur. Because responsibility is an abstract term, it must be defined for children by adults pointing out examples of it on television, in their home, and in their community. It must be differentiated from irresponsible behavior and actions at the same time. When an irresponsible action occurs or is observed, it is important to ask and remind the student what should have occurred instead.

How many times is responsibility equated with basic manners in our society and schools today? Students who appear irresponsible are usually not considering the rights of others and are frequently sent to the principal or counselor because of inappropriate actions. One sixth-grade girl who was repeatedly in the principal's office for being rude, bossy, and irresponsible said, "My teacher keeps telling me to mind my manners, but no one will tell me what they are." That comment was all the motivation that the principal and counselor needed to lead the teachers in a school-wide unit on manners. They saw drastic and positive changes in behavior when students understood how they were expected to behave. When adults explain how to behave instead saying "Don't do that," students learn how to act responsibly.

Responsibility is a learned behavior that becomes a part of children's personality when they have the opportunities and the freedom to make choices, demonstrate the decision-making process, and evaluate their actions. The normal progression of child development allows for increasing responsibility. Responsibility is learned when children have the freedom to experience the consequences of their actions. Student who cannot get ready for school in the morning may miss the bus and have to walk. They may have to stay after school to make up work that they missed by being tardy. Adolescents, who have increasing amounts of freedom, learn responsibility when there are natural and logical consequences to their behavior. Those who do not clean their rooms and put dirty clothes in the laundry may have to do their own laundry or not have clean clothes for school or a special event.

Children become confused about responsibility as their experiences and peer groups expand. What is thought of as responsible behavior in one home may not even be required in another where the parents do everything or nothing for the child. As students enter preadolescence they begin to wonder who is right. What is the correct behavior? Why do families do things so differently? One eighth-grade boy complained to his parents because he could not eat dinner in front of the TV in the family room. His parents firmly believed in family dinners where manners and conversation prevailed. When he visited his friend's house, he never saw the parents, and the children were allowed to eat wherever they wanted.

Children learn responsibility in groups and social situations. A seventh-grade class asked the principal if they could be responsible for planning and holding a dance at their school. They were given parameters of expected behavior for all attendees and required to have at least ten chaperones. Also, students had to follow all school rules at the dance. The students eagerly planned for music, food, and chaperones. They decided to have everyone bring in canned goods for the local food pantry. They put up posters and advertised the dance in all school publications. They insisted that they did not need adult intervention in the planning sessions. They thought they were acting responsibly until the day of the dance when they realized they had not reserved the gym for that night and a community basketball league was holding a tournament there. The wise principal did not cancel the basketball tournament and let the students, who had to hold their dance in a small school cafeteria, deal with the consequences. They learned that responsibility is developed with the assistance and modeling of others.

What Teachers Can Do to Help Students Develop Responsibility

1 Teachers can model responsible behavior and point out other models of responsible behavior in the school and in society.

2 Teachers can set expectations clearly so students know exactly what is expected of them.

3 Teachers can take a look around their classroom and ask themselves "What percentage of my students in this class
- accept responsibility for doing their work and handing it in on time?"
- get themselves ready for school and arrive on time?"
- act appropriately and responsibly in the classroom?"
- can initiate an activity and follow through until it's completed?"
- are helpful to others in the class?"
- ask for help when it is needed?"
- would be responsible in an emergency?"
- take responsibility for their actions?"

If more than 20 percent of the students consistently do not behave responsibly, teachers should examine the possible reasons with the school counselor or a social worker. Teachers can invite one of these professionals to observe the students in their class and suggest ways to help students gain responsibility.

4 Teachers can develop a classroom definition of responsibility, list all the responsibilities of being a member of the class, and display the list where students can refer to it daily.

5 Teachers can reward responsible behavior with classroom privileges. For example, if students get all their homework done and signed by parents for two weeks, they earn a homework pass.

6 Teachers can assign students to journal about their behavior each week and write about how they handled problems. Teachers would review several students' journals each week and have students take them home to share with parents.

7 Teachers can establish a random-acts-of-kindness program in their classroom that encourages students to help others.

8 Teachers can use stuffed animals in the elementary school, eggs in the middle school, and baby dolls or rag dolls in the high school to institute the responsibility project. Each student is given an object and they are to take it everywhere they go for a week and return it safely to class the following week. They are to log where they went and what they did with the object for a week. They are to be totally responsible for the safety and well-being of either the animal, egg, or baby doll.

9 Teachers can set up an assembly-line project in the classroom. Each student is responsible for a specific task, and all the tasks must be accomplished to complete the project. When the project is finished, the class can discuss why each role was essential. Craft projects work well in an assembly line, as do small cooking projects that have a recipe.

10 Teachers can ask students to watch a television show or movie for at least one hour and log all of the examples of positive and negative responsibility. The students can share their examples with the class and list them on the board. Then the class can discuss what role the media plays in helping or hindering problem solving. (See sample activity on page 96.)

11 Teachers can give students the A Responsible Person Would worksheet (see page 95) and have them answer the questions from each case study with a partner. Discuss their selections and reasons for choosing as they

did. Ask them to discuss the questions with an adult, log their answers, and share the responses with the class the next day.

12 Teachers can obtain a classroom pet that students are responsible for. Teachers should check the school policy on classroom pets and find out if any of the students have pet allergies. If there are limitations, teachers can try to get at least a fish bowl with goldfish. The students should research the options, how to obtain the pet, how to care for it, the cost, and possible complications. Teachers can post a chart listing all of the weekly jobs and the student responsible for each one.

13 Teachers can have students plant a school garden that benefits the school and community. Students can plant an herb garden indoors in pots or flowers and vegetables outdoors.

14 Teachers can read stories about responsible behavior to students. *Bartholomew and the Oobleck* by Dr. Seuss deals with responsible actions and is a good discussion starter for all age groups. Have students do an Internet search for stories, poems, and books about responsibility.

15 Teachers can assign students to read a biography about a famous person and write about that person's responsible actions.

16 Teachers can create a jobs board for the classroom that is easy to read and has a place to put index cards with jobs and students' names. Jobs that often appear on a jobs board include the following:
  ◆ furniture movers (put up chairs and straighten desks)
  ◆ paper collectors
  ◆ media assistants
  ◆ greeters (stand at the door and welcome everyone to class with a smile and handshake)
  ◆ errand runners
  ◆ decorators (who are responsible for a bulletin board that represents high interest topics for students).

Each student in the class must do every job at least once during the semester and can choose to repeat a job once they have done all of the jobs. Students may laugh or feel awkward and may try to avoid being greeters, but all students are taught the manners of entering a room and responding to a greeting.

17 Teachers can plan a free NASA simulation (http://imedia.ksc.nasa.gov/index1.html) with students and parents. This simulation provides an active learning experience with a strong emphasis on technology and offers many lessons on the different responsibilities of a space crew.

18 Teachers can teach responsibility and the law by setting up a classroom court (with a jury, judge, and lawyers) and having students role play cases that portray irresponsible behavior. Each trial should end with the students identifying the responsible behavior. Afterwards, students can search the Internet for local and state laws regarding responsible behavior. Teachers can videotape each trial to show future classes. When available, lawyer volunteers can answer written questions about each case. (See case studies on page 98.)

19 Teachers can divide an upcoming unit into small lessons and have each student plan and implement a five-minute lesson on some skill, concept, or attitude presented in the material. Teachers should provide students with a lesson plan format and encourage them to use a variety of approaches to teach the lesson. Classmates offer constructive feedback on each lesson as it is given. As a follow-up activity, students can write about how it felt to be responsible for that lesson.

20 Teachers can help students understand the many kinds of responsibility required in the school by having them complete the worksheet on page 100.

21 Teachers can hold a poster contest requiring students to design posters about the topic: Responsible Actions, Responsible People.

22 Teachers can divide students into groups and have them write a song about being responsible. Students can use any familiar tune and write lyrics. All groups should sing their song for the class.

23 Teachers can have students write and produce a play about responsible and irresponsible behaviors. Teachers should involve all students by having groups responsible for writing, acting, stage design, props, costumes, advertising, and programs. Students can sign up for the responsibility they want in this assignment. All students should participate in some manner.

24 Teachers can use the independent study project from Chapter 3 to teach both resourcefulness and responsibility

25 Teachers can teach goal setting and decision making with an emphasis on responsible personal action, consequences, and alternatives. (See activities in Chapter 3.)

26 Teachers can reinforce responsible actions by class members by having all students fill out the Responsible Classmate Questionnaire (see page 101). Have students share one or two of their selections and explain why they chose the responsible person that they did for each question.

What Administrators Can Do to Help Students Develop Responsibility

1. Administrators can establish a student advisory board that meets on a weekly basis with the administrative team. The membership of this advisory board should rotate on a quarterly basis so many student voices are heard.

2. At the first staff meeting in October, administrators should ask teachers to list the ten students in their class(es) who they feel need to work on responsibility. The administrators combine the lists and create a challenge list for teachers of the top ten or twenty most frequently named students. Then those students are paired with teachers for mentoring. Teachers should select from the list a student with whom they have developed a rapport. Mentors meet weekly with their students for a one-on-one conference.

3. Administrators can work with teachers to establish community-service projects where students and teachers can work together to finish a project responsibly. This can also be an extra-curricular activity for students.

4. Administrators can recognize and reward responsible students with Student of the Week, Month, or Semester rewards.

5. Administrators can help staff determine the school's definition of responsibility so that teacher expectations are consistent and age appropriate.

6. Administrators can work with students to identify and adopt a community organization that needs help. Students can earn service points for graduation by working for that organization on weekends or vacations. The key is to establish a relationship and understanding between the school and the organization so that students are clear on what they are expected to do.

7. Administrators can surprise students with a reward such as a Friday afternoon movie for responsible behavior over an extended period of time.

8. Administrators can allow students to give the morning announcements or start a student television show that includes essential information about school.

9. Administrators can provide teachers with materials and training that will help students become increasingly more responsible. (See pages 95–101.)

10 Administrators can provide parents with information about building responsible behavior in the home.

11 Administrators can establish a monthly responsible-citizen award for a student who is nominated in writing by teachers and/or students. This award should be for ongoing responsible behavior, helping individuals, or helping the community. It should be announced in both the school newspaper and a letter to parents.

12 Administrators can connect responsibility with privileges in the school by allowing students to earn the right to go on field trips, do special projects, and gain rewards.

13 Administrators can catch students being good citizens by noting their behavior and then calling them to the office for a congratulatory chat. At-risk students might receive recognition simply for being in attendance for a week or more. Administrators can note their efforts and let the students know that they support them.

14 Administrators can set aside a Responsible Citizen week, offering posters, books, and media about responsibility in every class. Responsible community members, including those popular with at-risk kids (like chefs, auto mechanics, police officers, doctors, builders, radio announcers, athletes, and business owners), can speak to groups of students about their job responsibilities. By focusing on responsibility for a week, students begin to understand the abstract concept.

15 If possible, administrators can take students to an outdoor education group training experience. The kids who are having the most trouble in school can use their talents and skills in an out-of-school challenge event, thus improving their self-image.

16 Administrators can print parent suggestions that focus on developing responsibility in the school newsletter or include them on the school Web site.

What Parents Can Do to Help Students Develop Responsibility

1 Parents can give children small jobs from the time they understand the concept of helping. When they ask, "May I help with the dishes?" the answer should be *yes*. Some early childhood specialists blame the electric dishwasher for lack of responsibility in some students. They contend

that convenience appliances have robbed children of small tasks that they could learn to do and be responsible for.

2 Parents can provide children with a quiet place to do their homework and expect them to have it done by a certain time at night.

3 Parents can create a family jobs chart and post it on the refrigerator with everyone's jobs in writing. Family members can change jobs or trade jobs by using Post-it notes on the chart.

4 Parents can restrict and monitor family Internet use. Even the most responsible child is often naive about the dangers that can arise from improper use.

5 Parents can hold meetings to celebrate responsible behavior or discuss family decisions.

6 Parents can point out the consequences of irresponsible behavior and discuss what a responsible person would do in the same situation. One mom tried for months to get her son to clean his room, his only family responsibility, but he would clean only part of his room halfheartedly. She finally found an effective solution. One day he needed to go to baseball practice two miles away, so he asked his mom to drive him. She drove one mile and made him walk the rest of the way while she followed. He experienced the consequences of her doing half of what he needed and made the connection between responsible behavior and consequences.

7 Parents can ask children to talk about what they should do when asked to be responsible for something at school.

8 Parents can give children the facts about issues like drugs, alcohol, sex, and gangs. Parents can pass along their values and help children gather accurate information.

9 Parents can get their kids a library card and take them to the library. Children learn the responsibility of caring for books, returning them on time, and using computers to search for books.

10 Parents can share with teachers information about their children's increasing or unusual family responsibilities. They should share information about the child that might affect how the teachers perceive his or her level of responsibility. They should consider the following types of questions: Are adolescents responsible for getting younger children in the family ready for school? Are younger children responsible for getting the evening meal for the family? Is someone moving in or out of the home that might affect everyone's level of responsibility?

11 Parents can encourage children to be involved in community groups that teach responsibility such as clubs, sports teams, or youth volunteer programs.

12 Parents can encourage children to help others in school, their neighborhood, and the community by involving students in helping senior citizens, volunteering for projects, and caring for plants and animals.

13 Parents can point out examples of responsible behavior in the news, on television, and in stories.

14 Parents can read children's stories aloud that focus on responsible actions.

15 Parents can stay involved with their children's school and classroom teacher(s). They should know what the teacher's expectations are and what the assignments are so that they can provide a supportive environment.

16 Parents can adopt an elderly friend at a nursing home or retirement center and let their children decide how to befriend and help this person.

17 If their children seem irresponsible for their ages, parents can consider the following evaluative questions:
- Is this behavior ongoing or occasional?
- Does this behavior upset others or cause conflict? Are the children given opportunities to be responsible and learn from mistakes?
- Do the children know what they are supposed to be doing in each situation?
- Are the responsibility expectations appropriate for the ages of the children?
- Do the children become responsible when the behavior is brought to their attention?

18 Parents can state family rules clearly and in positive terms and model how to follow the rules.

19 Parents can allow children to experience the consequences of their actions.

20 Parents can resist being overly controlling or overly permissive. Instead, they can give children some freedom within clearly defined limits with clearly defined consequences.

21 Parents can praise responsible behavior.

Summary

Responsibility is a learned behavior, developed when given opportunities to see models of responsible behavior, opportunities to practice responsible behavior, and recognition of growth towards responsible actions. Parents, teachers, and administrators can provide opportunities for students to practice responsible behaviors from the time they enter preschool until they graduate. Responsible-behavior activities should be planned and implemented in every classroom and throughout the school. The school staff should discuss the term responsibility and come to an agreement on how to help students understand the concept and the actions. Parents, teachers, and administrators can work together to identify expectations and clarify those expectations for the students. The basic question is: What does it mean to be a responsible person in this school?

References and Resources

References

Bergmann, S., Brough, J. and Shepard, D. (2009). *Teach my kid I dare you*. Larchmont, New York: Eye On Education.

Carney, S. (November 16, 2007). Lesson plan: Taking responsibility: helping kids lose the excuses and make better choices. Retrieved from <www.suite101.com/content/lesson-plan-taking-responsibility-a35594#ixzz1M3nBupLI>

NASA Interactive Media <http://imedia.ksc.nasa.gov/index1.html>

Resources

Character counts! is the incorporation of common language and terms into families, organizations, agencies, and schools. It uses the six pillars of trustworthiness, responsibility, caring, respect, fairness, and citizenship to describe how a person of character thinks and behaves. This character education program includes free lesson plans on the six pillars for all age levels. The lessons for responsibility are integrated with the content for middle and high school teachers. <www.charactercounts.org> <www.goodcharacter.com>

Choices series, Tom Snyder Productions, for one-computer classrooms. This program focuses on how to make decisions and take responsibility. <www.tomsnyder.com>

Educators for Social Responsibility offers lesson plans. <www.esrnational.org>

Scholastic *Instructor Magazine*. Teacher-created activities for teaching responsibility. <www2.scholastic.com/browse/article.jsp?id=11536&print=1>

The Teacher's Corner. Lots of ideas and reproducibles. <www.theteacherscorner.net>

Strategies, Lessons, and Activities for Teaching
RESPONSIBILITY

A Responsible Person Would...

Step 1: Place students in pairs and have them answer these questions.

Problem 1: You find a set of car keys in the school hallway. They have no identification on them. A responsible person would

_____

_____

Problem 2: Your mom is sick with the flu, and everything at home is a mess. You have a big science test tomorrow. A responsible person would

_____

_____

Problem 3: You have homework to do and a soccer game right after school. A responsible person would

_____

_____

Problem 4: You overhear a group of older students planning to paint graffiti on the school that night. A responsible person would

_____

_____

Problem 5: You missed the team bus because you could not find your uniform shorts in your messy room. A responsible person would

_____

_____

Step 2: Have students discuss their answers and reasons for choosing what they did.

Step 3: Have students discuss the questions with an adult and write their responses.

Step 4: Share the responses in class.

What Television Teaches Us About Responsibility

Directions: Choose a television show that has more than one character and is not a cartoon. It should have multiple characters and last at least one hour.

Step 1: Log all of the examples of negative and positive responsibility.

1. Name of show(s):

    _____

2. What was the show about? (one or two sentences)

    _____

    _____

3. Who were the main characters?

    _____

    _____

4. Write one example of responsible behavior for each of the main characters.

    _____

    _____

    _____

    _____

5. Write one or more examples of irresponsible behavior by someone on the show.

    _____

    _____

    _____

    _____

6. What problem(s) did the characters encounter?

_____

_____

_____

_____

7. How was (were) the problem(s) solved?

_____

_____

_____

_____

8. How do you define responsibility?

_____

_____

_____

_____

9. What did you learn about responsibility from watching this show?

_____

_____

_____

_____

Step 2: Share examples in class and list them on the board.

Step 3: Discuss how media affects our problem solving.

Role Play: Classroom Law Trials for Irresponsible Behavior

Directions:

Appoint the following roles in the classroom:

    2 lawyers

    12 jury members

    1 judge

    Each lawyer, jury member, and judge is responsible for gathering information, making his or her own decision, and stating an opinion during the trial.

The jury must decide if the students broke the law, what law they broke, and what the consequences should be. The judge makes sure that all parties participate and delivers the sentence. The rest of the class is responsible for stating what other decisions the defendants could have made. After the trial, discuss as a class what responsible actions should have been taken in each case.

Elementary-School Classroom:

Mr. and Mrs. Sorry have a very large, mean dog. The dog is allowed to run throughout the neighborhood, jump on people, and knock down little children. It tips over garbage cans and spreads garbage all over neighbors' yards. If anyone tells it to stop, it turns, growls, and shows its teeth. It seems to be very hungry and barks constantly. Mr. and Mrs. Sorry will not answer their phone or door and do not talk to other people. The neighbors are tired of their irresponsible behavior and decide to call the police.

Middle-School Classroom

R.J. and C.T. are eighth graders who are angry because they have to stay after school to make up work with a new tutor. If they don't make up the work, they will be suspended. They really want to go to a skateboard rally in the park and see some girls from another school. In the hallway before last period, they threaten two seventh-grade boys that if they do not go to tutoring, pretend to be them, and do their make-up work, they will hurt them the next day and tell the principal that they have been stealing in school. If they tell on them, the older boys will spread lies about them on the Internet. The seventh-graders are terrified and decide go to tutoring for the bullies. The new tutor recognizes them as imposters and tells the principal.

High-School Classroom

Scenario 1: Martin needs $75 to buy the used car he has been saving for. He cannot wait to have his own car. His grandmother is ill and asks him to go to the bank for her and gives him $200 to deposit. He knows that she does not always remember numbers correctly and deposits only $100. He buys his car and some gas for it. His grandmother asks him for the deposit slip. He lies and says she only gave him $100. She catches him in the lie because she wrote down what she gave him.

Scenario 2: Samantha goes to school every day and attends her morning classes. At lunch time she leaves school and goes to a friend's house to hang out and drink beer. One afternoon she gets too drunk to go home and gets sick all over the furniture and carpet. She breaks a table and small chair while falling over them. One of her afternoon teachers is concerned because she is failing a required college-prep course and calls Samantha's parents to see why she is not in school in the afternoons. She tells her parents that she is in school, but her schedule has been changed so she no longer has that class this year. Her friend's parents call Samantha's parents to ask for money to have the carpet and furniture cleaned. When they insist that their daughter was in school and could not have ruined the furniture, the other parents call a lawyer.

Responsibility in Our School

Step 1: Pair students and have them write on the following chart the names of the people who work in the school.

Step 2: Have students list each person's job responsibilities.

Step 3: Have students write why each job is important to the school.

Step 4: Combine pairs of students into groups of four to share their lists and create one composite list.

Step 5: Assign each group to make up four questions to ask a person who works in the school.

Step 6: Put a sign-up sheet on the board for groups to list their interviewees. (Only one interview per school employee.)

Step 7: Have groups share their questions and lists with the class.

Step 8: After the interviews, have groups report on the responsibilities of the people who work in the school.

Responsibility in Our School

People who work at the school	Responsibility	Why their job is important

Interview questions

1. _____

_____

_____

_____

2. _____

_____

_____

_____

3. _____

_____

_____

_____

4. _____

_____

_____

_____

Responsible Classmate Questionnaire

Have students complete a questionnaire like this one several times during the school year.

1. If you needed help with spelling, whom would you ask?

2. If you needed to build something like a go-cart, whom would you choose to help you?

3. If you wanted to write a song with someone, whom would you choose?

4. If you were lost in the woods, who would be best at helping you find your way out?

5. If your class wanted to enter a contest, who would organize them to enter the contest?

6. If you wanted to be sure that you understood the material before a big science test, whom would you call?

7. If you were sad and needed someone to listen, to whom would you turn?

8. If the school wanted an under-the-sea mural in the hallway, who could paint it?

9. If a reporter wanted someone to represent your class for a newspaper article or a television interview, whom would you pick?

10. If you were to choose someone to lead your class, whom would it be?

11. If you were going to see someone in a comedy show, whom would it be?

12. If you were to name the student who knows the most about geography and the world, whom would it be?

13. If you were to name the best weatherperson, whom would it be?

14. If you had to pick a person to train for a race with, whom would it be?

15. If you wanted to eat healthier, whom would you choose to help you remember what to eat?

16. If you wanted to be sure to get any job done on time and correctly, whom would you choose to work with?

When the students have completed their list, have students take turns sharing one person from their list and tell why they chose that person. Have a class discussion about why people's ability to be responsible depends on the task they are being asked to do. Ask students to write in their journals. You can give them the following sentence starters:

As a result of this activity, I learned that…

As a result of this activity, I learned that I…

5

Helping Students Develop Positive
RELATIONSHIPS

*"Piglet sidled up to Pooh from behind. 'Pooh!' he
whispered. 'Yes, Piglet?' 'Nothing,' said Piglet, taking
Pooh's paw. 'I just wanted to be sure of you.'"*

A.A. Milne

What Defines Positive Relationships?

Everyone knows what relationships are, but what defines effective relationships between teachers and students? Educational literature and research are definitive that students must grow to trust their teachers and feel that mutual respect exists. Students must learn to work together in school if they wish to be successful in adulthood.

Positive relationships within a school create a positive atmosphere, making the school a place where students want to be and learn. There are several types of relationships for educators and parents to consider when they try to assist kids who are struggling. Along with the teacher-student relationships are the student-to-student relationships, the parent–teacher relationships, and the parent-student relationships. If any one of those relationships is struggling, the students' learning will be affected. The best teachers in the school cannot inspire students to come to school if there are peer problems or students feel unsafe in the environment. A comfortable social climate may bring students to school but not to class. One high school student stated, "I just go to the classes of the teachers that I know, know me, and care about me. The rest just don't matter." In addition, if parents do not feel comfortable with the school, they will not support their child's learning.

Learning is a social event. Relationships among teachers and students not only matter; positive relationships are critical, more so than the educational program, the curriculum or any instructional strategies. As Marzano (2003) said, "Teachers' actions in their classrooms have twice the impact on student achievement as do school policies regarding curriculum, assessment, staff collegiality, and community involvement." That statement is worth reading again. What the teacher does impacts students' academic success more than other critical factors. Many students, especially those with high needs, tend to have poor images of themselves as learners. They need to perceive that their teachers have faith in them and genuinely care about their success. Even in a standards-driven and assessment-driven school culture, positive relationships among teachers and students are important, perhaps even more so. We want students to bond to the school and to try to do their best on required local and state exams. Students who feel alienated and lack confidence in their abilities have no reason to try to do well in the classroom or on assessments.

Every student, *every* day must have at least one meaningful interaction with a teacher. Only by creating a genuine culture of support and caring will educators be able to crack open the students' rough exteriors and spark their internal motivation to succeed. And those students who are the most difficult to build a good relationship with are probably those who need it the most.

To ensure that these critical relationships are valued, established, maintained, and assessed, many schools that serve at-risk youngsters set up advising or mentoring programs. Educators can't all bond with all kids. Mentoring requires a special kind of relationship. Mentoring programs should include a process that matches each student with a teacher with whom they can bond. That teacher becomes the student's advisor or mentor and works with other teachers and the student's family. Educators must commit to establishing these relationships. (See Figure 5.1.)

What Teachers Can Do to Help Students Develop Positive Peer Relationships

1 Teachers can take the time to do a get-acquainted activity at the beginning of the year or new term. This is essential to developing a culture of respect among the students. Teachers should participate with the students in the activity so that the classroom is seen as a community, not as a threat to vulnerable students. (See samples on page 122.)

2 Teachers can use small groups daily to solve problems, work on projects, discuss and review material, and generate assessments. When using small groups, teachers should start with pairs, and then combine pairs to make groups of four. Students who feel uncomfortable will more readily work with one other student in the beginning instead of a larger group.

Figure 5.1

The Mentor's Pledge

I commit to making a difference;
to support, guide, and be a role model.

I commit to being consistent;
to be a steady figure over time, to be persistent, and to help another persevere.

I commit to encouraging another;
by listening, by understanding, by fostering strengths, and by showing empathy.

I commit to building a mutual relationship;
to enter the world of someone else, to hear about new dreams and challenges,
to share my own stories, and to respect the differences between us.

I commit to asking for assistance;
when I need my own support, when the struggles of a child are bigger than I can
handle, when I am unsure.

I commit to recognizing;
that change often comes in small steps that barely leave footprints, that victories
are often unseen or unspoken, and that obstacles will always be present.

I commit to remaining sympathetic;
to the storms weathered, to the adversity faced, and to the experiences that
occurred long before this child entered my life.

I commit to realizing;
that my actions carry new weight and responsibility, that my role can never be
taken lightly, that my life will also change with this experience.

I commit to being a mentor.

Source: Mentoring.org (http://www.mentoring.org), published by the National Mentoring Partnership,
covers issues on youth mentoring. Used by permission.

3 Teachers can use hands-on projects and labs that require the use of a
variety of student talents. Students with reading problems may have no
trouble with logic, puzzles, or physical challenges.

4 Teachers can teach students about Howard Gardner's work with multiple intelligences (www.howardgardner.com) so they learn to see their
peers as multifaceted individuals instead of one dimensional.

5 Teachers can structure room seating so that students can see each other
during discussions. It is more difficult for students to discuss something with classmates while they are looking at their backs. Discussions

RELATIONSHIPS

should be among students rather than between the teacher and one student at a time. Teachers can show students how to discuss ideas by offering mini-topics for short brainstorming sessions. A fun starter topic might be "If students our age ran the world, we would...."

Teachers can prepare for occasions when students have a "blow up" in their classroom. Once in a while, relationships among students reach the crisis stage for individual students, which can affect the entire class and learning for the day. The Individual Crisis Intervention and De-Escalation Model on page 124 is an effective tool for dealing with this type of situation.

What Teachers Can Do to Develop Positive Relationships with Students

1 Teachers can consider the climate of their classroom and make students feel welcome. Do they *want* to be in class, or do they dread going there? If students feel negatively about a school, class, or teacher in general, it will be a struggle to get those students to pay attention, comply with rules and procedures, or try to succeed academically. Teachers can try the following strategies:

- ◆ Look into school or class absences or tardies. Frequent absence is an immediate red flag. Try to find out the reason for a student's absence or tardiness as soon as you notice it. Does the youngster have an illness or are other problems at play? You can counteract the problem once you determine *why* a student doesn't show up or is chronically late. Showing concern about students' attendance shows them that you value their presence. Don't hesitate to ask a student how you can help him or her to attend more regularly. One middle school student who was late to school every day was walking his elementary school-aged sister to her school each morning. What a responsible youngster! Yet, in many places, he would be punished for his tardiness. Instead, the effective school discovers the reason for his behavior.

- ◆ Provide positive greetings, some small talk, and good eye contact. Try to be welcoming to all students—even if you wish they were absent. Think about what others do to make you feel welcome to a new group and use those same kinds of tactics with your kids. For some students, the time they spend with a caring teacher may be the most reassuring time of their day. Show concern for and knowledge of their activities and interests in and out of school. Ask how they're doing and listen to their responses.

- ◆ Establish an authoritative teaching style. Baumrind (1971) described the difference between authoritarian and authoritative parenting styles. These styles can be translated to teachers as well. Authoritarian styles are more controlling and expect compliance without question. Authoritative styles convey messages of high expectations but with apparent support (being equally demanding as warm and responsive). Authoritative styles more often breed self-confidence and independence in youngsters, while authoritarian behaviors can cause anxiety and a lack of self-confidence. Try to give students reasons for expectations and offer your support.

◆ Solicit student feedback. Educators evaluate students all the time. Students appreciate a chance to give feedback to their teachers. This opportunity tells the students that the teachers respect their opinions and really want to help their students to succeed. (Sample feedback questions are on page 121.)

2 Some of the characteristics of effective student-teacher relationships involve the culture of classroom instruction. As a more diverse population of youngsters enters our schools, it becomes necessary to understand and design ways to meet individual student needs. Whole group instruction must be balanced with small group and individual learning time. Teachers should consider the following ideas:

◆ Provide clear purpose for the task. Students, especially those who are not trusting of the school organization, need to know that what they are doing in school matters. So often, reluctant learners see no purpose to the curriculum and no connection between what they are learning and real life. "What are we learning this for anyway" becomes a familiar mantra. Think about your own reaction to a graduate class, for example, or a professional development workshop. Don't you want to know what the purpose is for any effort or time you might expend? Kids who trust their teachers and the system may readily comply with curricular demands, but those who are less trusting or confident will balk at demands without a clearly defined purpose. So often underachieving students are given mundane work—worksheets, drill, and practice—which is precisely the opposite of what they need. Underachievers can be motivated when presented with interesting, important, or creative tasks. They, too, need to be challenged, but they need to know that someone is there to help when they are in need. Try to get in the habit of telling students the importance of what they are studying. "You need this information because it's on the test" is *not* a motivator. Underachievers are often not concerned about what's on a test. Look at your curriculum requirements and figure out why the information is important. Ask around, google it, reflect on it. If you can't figure out why your students must master a certain concept, bring it up at a departmental or faculty meeting. If content has no valid purpose, it may need to be deleted from the curriculum.

◆ Provide strong and clear guidance regarding academics and behavior. Kids need to know specifically what they're supposed to do and how to act. Rubrics really help and can be used for both academic and behavioral expectations, plus they can be individualized! Teachers often tell students to "behave." What does that mean? Especially kids who hail from chaotic households need to know how some of these abstract terms translate into actions. For example, teachers, particularly in elementary- and middle-school levels, may want to discuss what responsibility looks like and sounds like in the classroom, keeping in mind that many students are concrete learners.

◆ Define clear expectations and learning goals by using rubrics and allowing flexibility with individualized goals. What does it mean to be "on grade level"? How will each student get there? What are the necessary steps? Too often a goal seems so unattainable. Those of you who live in a home with a yard and landscaping, think about how you feel during those first days of spring when you realize how much yard work really needs to be done. It can seem overwhelming to the point where you just go back inside the house. But if you set specific and attainable goals and steps to reach them, the task becomes much more manageable. And remember that students have different learning styles and temperaments, so not all students can follow the same path at the same speed. It is academic and behavioral progress that we want to see, so focus on personal learning goals rather than on whole-class goals. Most children want to be seen as individuals rather than being compared to others. "I'll never be as good as Andre, so why should I even try" is a deadly perception.

◆ Encourage students to set some of their own objectives. People want to have some control over their world. Permit students to set some of their own objectives for a unit of instruction. They may even design ways to approach their own learning. This tactic not only helps students to feel some ownership for their educations, but also assists them in thinking through their own interests and needs. Self-designed objectives and self-assessments lead to higher-level thinking and responsibility for a person's own learning. Student-led conferences are quite effective in helping students to self-assess realistically.

3 Vulnerable students often have behavioral issues. Sometimes they come to school wary of authority figures or organizational systems. Many at-risk students feel out of control at a time when they are trying to develop autonomy and self-identity. Teachers can scrutinize the way they treat students in order to encourage appropriate school behavior. Yelling, sarcasm, threatening and authoritarian control do *not* work in

the long run. Teachers don't benefit when students are afraid of them. Furthermore, learning can't occur when students feel afraid. Remember that the second step of Maslow's Hierarchy of Needs is a feeling of safety (see Maslow's Hierarchy in Chapter 1). Maslow found that students who were deficient in physiological, safety, belonging, or esteem needs could not achieve their full potentials. Consider the following ideas for classroom management:

♦ Involve students in developing clear rules and procedures by having class discussions that establish mutual consent. Students need to feel that they are part of a positive school culture that values their voices. If they help establish the rules and procedures, they will more likely understand and adhere to them. Also, you can have a more meaningful discussion with students who do not follow the policies they helped design. A middle school teacher in Las Vegas felt like she was over her head with discipline problems. Over the winter break, she studied classroom management theories and strategies. On the first day back to school, she held class meetings. She told students that she knew that the class was too chaotic for learning to occur and she needed their help. Each class worked in small groups to design classroom expectations, which they presented to the whole class. They settled on a few understandable, concrete, and important rules. Not used to being consulted, most students were eager to have a say. The teacher reported that the change in *her* behavior resulted in a positive change in the students' behavior. She had moved from authoritarian to authoritative control—and it worked!

♦ Move strategically around the classroom. When students are off task or confused, they are more likely to disrupt the class. Many kids are reluctant to ask a question or make a comment. By moving around the classroom, teachers can stay within close proximity to all students, allowing each a chance to engage teachers more privately. Teacher movement keeps students on task and inspires students to think twice before being disruptive.

♦ Help students feel valued by giving them ownership for their ideas. When students feel valued, they are more likely to behave in class. If a student answers a question correctly or makes an interesting point, give them credit for it. Be careful not to take a student's answer and turn it into your own by elaborating or clarifying. Let *them* do it. Then refer to their remark as "Susie's point." Try not to repeat a student's answer. Instead, ask him/her to repeat it or ask another student to put the answer into his/her own words. When teachers consistently repeat students' answers, students become less likely to listen to each other. Put the learning in the hands of the students. Facilitate and guide rather than tell and control.

◆ Encourage participation from all students. When students are actively involved in a lesson, they are less likely to be distracted (or to distract others). Vygotsky (1978) identified the connection between young people's language and their thinking. He noted that silencing children's language could result in silencing their thoughts. Although he was referring specifically to young children, educators realize that participation helps all students to pay attention, to reflect on what is being taught, and to illuminate possible misunderstandings. Rather than relying on a few students to contribute, use gimmicks to get all students to participate in class discussions and activities. For example, give each student three pennies and tell them that by the end of class they must have "spent" each of their pennies by contributing something to the class. Each contribution equals a penny spent. In younger grades, try putting students' names on popsicle sticks that they have decorated. When asking questions, pull out a popsicle stick and call on its owner. If you work with older students, you can write their names on slips of paper to pull out of a basket. (The names should go back in the basket so students won't think that one answer or comment lets them off the hook.) Make it an expectation that each student must contribute something every class period.

◆ Conduct one-on-one conferences. Such conferencing techniques help to build trust, which can affect students' behavior positively. From time to time, try to talk individually with your students, especially with those who need you most. One-on-ones needn't last a long time; three or four minutes can be quality time well spent. Ask questions like "How are you doing with the goals you set?" "Do you have any questions?" "What can I do to support your progress?" Take the time to *listen* to the student rather than talk. Go into the one-on-one with a few planned key questions and take notes. Then follow up with the student's requests or concerns. At-risk students often perceive teachers as not listening to them. Specific one-on-one time can alleviate that perception. During individual interactions with students, try physically to get on their level. Instead of standing and hovering above them, squat or sit down and meet them eye to eye. This action levels the playing field in the students' eyes.

◆ Distribute feedback notes and notes of appreciation. These forms of communication help students stay on task. Try not to omit feedback until it's time for formal progress reports or report cards. Jot a few notes to your students. Using a composition book, teachers can write comments on the left-hand page and students can write comments on the right-hand page. If you write "please try to get your homework in on time," note it when the student complies. Teachers can use this communication device to work with the design of learning or behavior goals for individual students. Reinforce positive efforts.

◆ View classroom management as instructive rather than punitive. It takes a while to master any skill. Some students don't know what appropriate behaviors look or sound like. Teach them, then give them feedback. Everyone makes mistakes. The goal is to help students to self-regulate. Punishment without instruction doesn't stick. Think about adults who speed down the highway until they see a police car. They slow down until the trooper is out of sight, then press on the accelerator again. We want students to behave appropriately *even when adults aren't looking.* That kind of behavior entails consistent instruction with feedback and support. Ask questions like "What else could you have done in that situation?" and "How could you have approached that situation differently?" Punishment without instruction does not alter behavior in the long run.

4 Build the perception that teachers are supportive and respectful. Merely giving a student a zero for incomplete homework or a failing grade on a test doesn't provide academic support. If the homework was important to do, make sure that each student does it, even if it's completed in school rather than at home (but closely examine all assignments to ensure that they really *are* necessary). If a student fails to master a unit of instruction and the teacher just moves on, what message does that send to the student? They perceive that it just doesn't matter and they become less likely to try on the next unit. Show students that teachers have faith in them and that their efforts matter. Don't give them easy work; that sends a message that teachers have little or no faith in their abilities. Challenge them; communicate with them when they have difficulties or fail to complete a task. Ask *why* they couldn't complete it. Help them to find a way to succeed. Perhaps the home environment is one where the student can't work independently. In that case, provide an alternative.

5 Teachers can build a reason for optimism so students don't fear failure (especially if they're accustomed to it). Students need to perceive that teachers have confidence in them and their abilities. So many at-risk students feel out of control and hopeless. Lack of achievement is not the same as lack of ability. Students' negative behaviors are often a coping mechanism ("I don't care about this task anyway, so why should I try," or "I don't know how to do this, so why bother"). In order to tackle difficult tasks, people must feel that there is opportunity for success. People don't often adhere to plans that have no chance of success. Think about someone on a diet. If the weight fails to come off, how long does a person stick to it? We need concrete evidence that what we are doing makes a difference. Teachers can break units down into manageable parts, give feedback on progress at multiple points, and point out progress made. They should remember that motivation is not fixed; it can be altered and developed. Teachers shouldn't fall into the trap of listening to a former teacher's complaints about students or thinking that there's something

wrong with a student. McCombs and Pope (1994) said, "Many programs for high-risk youth are not having the necessary impact because they assume there is something to be fixed or something that is missing in these youth" (pp. 17–18). That attitude can easily cause a self-fulfilling prophecy. When students come into class, let them enter with a clean slate. If they make a mistake today, let them know that their teachers won't hold it against them tomorrow. Treat each day as a new opportunity for success. At the end of every day, both teachers and students should take time to reflect on what went right during the day rather than focusing on what went wrong. Smile and be optimistic. Optimism will go a long way to inoculating students against pessimism.

6 ▌ Teachers can demonstrate caring and concern for students' opinions and needs by offering students choices. Similar to self-setting of objectives, student choice allows students to feel some ownership of their learning. Individual rubrics can include various suggestions for students to show their mastery of a unit or concept. Allowing them a say in how they are assessed or what project they will complete motivates some students to at least try. Teachers should ask students what they are interested in and what they'd like to learn. Then, teachers can determine how to incorporate students' interests into the curriculum (it's surprising how often this will occur).

7 ▌ Teachers can offer genuine compliments (no sugar-coating, but noticing student strengths). They should tell the truth gently. Teachers should recognize progress students have made (they often do not see their own progress) and compliment them on their efforts. Certainly, teachers should let students know when they've made a mistake, but without blame. Kids don't purposely give a wrong answer. Teachers should find out what their logic is by asking, "What were you thinking about when you gave that answer?" Teachers must give them the benefit of the doubt that they were on the right track. Simply saying, "No, that's not the answer I was looking for. Who can help Ralph?" will shut down a student in lightning speed.

8 ▌ Teachers can recognize and reinforce acceptable behavior. Students note that teachers tend not to listen to them. They feel a sense of injustice when they are called out for misbehavior but not recognized for appropriate behavior. This is especially important for students who are just learning what *is* appropriate behavior in a classroom. Positive reinforcement helps them to keep trying to improve. Teachers must show students that they are paying attention to them.

9 ▌ Teachers can use prearranged signals to cue students. Of course, students need time to learn appropriate behaviors and they will make mistakes. A simple cuing technique, like a quick hand on the shoulder,

a thumbs-down, or a nose crinkle, can signal students to adjust their behavior without drawing attention to it with the rest of the class. This technique allows students to examine a behavior, learn to recognize it as inappropriate, and change it. Some students with diagnosed ADHD can't tell whether or not they're paying attention. A cue can help them to think about how they feel and what they are doing when they aren't paying attention and learn to self-adjust.

10 Teachers can discover student interests. Students want to be seen as people, not as numbers. They have interests inside and outside of school that may lead to development of expertise and a sense of worth. A student who obviously did not seem to fit in with his middle school peers started to shine when the school hosted a "show your talents" day. This particular student raised chickens at home and was actually able to breed a blue chicken. On talent day, he brought it in and explained a homemade chart that showed the dominant and recessive genes that he bred to produce this blue chicken. Peers and adults were amazed and the boy glowed with delight. In another example, a student teacher of remedial reading discovered that one of her reluctant students was fascinated with the Chevy Camaro. She used this information to provide interesting reading material for this student. He didn't hesitate to read and write about his passion. The point was that he was reading and writing, something he loathed to do previously. Find out what your students are interested in and use it to your advantage (and the student's advantage).

11 Teachers can connect with their students' homes. School personnel who develop successful programs for vulnerable youth understand the importance of frequent and positive home-school relationships. They work hard to involve families and adapt their practices to accommodate the families they serve. These teachers don't merely do the same old thing and expect parents to become involved. And, most importantly, they don't give up on the kids because of the actions or inactions of the parents! *Teach My Kid I Dare You: The Educator's Essential Guide to Parent Involvement* offers countless ideas to spark home involvement (Bergmann, Brough, and Shepard, 2008). Here are some ideas for connecting with the home.

   ◆ Identify the parents with whom you need to connect and learn more about them. Is English a problem for these parents? Do they work different shifts? Are school visitations difficult because there are toddlers at home? Can the parents help with their children's homework even if they can't show up at school functions? Do they know how to collaborate with school personnel? Assign one teacher to be the liaison to identified parents. Send home a questionnaire or call the parents to gather information about their children's interests and needs. Make sure parents know whom to contact at the school and how to reach that liaison.

◆ Plan parent involvement rather than leaving it to chance. Remember that it is the educators' job to design effective home-school partnerships. Family dynamics and characteristics have changed drastically over the last decade. We can't continue to plan home communications the way we've always done it. We must change to meet the needs of different kinds of families. Just because parents don't attend a school conference doesn't mean they don't care. Understand that there are many reasons why parents cannot or choose not to visit the school and adapt the parent-involvement program. Castigating the parents doesn't help students; meeting the families' needs does.

◆ Develop trusting home-school relationships by providing positive home communications. This one is simple. Too often the parents of at-risk students are bombarded with bad news without receiving any good news. If you communicate with the home to report students' mistakes, you should also communicate positive news. Most parents are doing the best that they can. Even if parents seem uninvolved, you should maintain communication. Most importantly, don't give up on children because their parents seem to lack interest and are uninvolved.

Teachers benefit from good relationships with students. The better the relationship, the better students' behavior and motivation will be. Taking time to build relationships will pay off by making for a more pleasant and non-confrontational atmosphere, thus making the educators' job more pleasant and rewarding. Plus, the idea that educators have impacted a child's life is a reward in and of itself. Reflect on the student author's meaning in the following poem (Figure 5.2). To be that teacher is what it's all about.

Figure 5.2

And Gladly Lerne

I trudge through endless halls
And sit in musty cubicles
   (only they're labs, most of them)
And gaze through someones
   (only they're no ones, most of them)
Who look over my head to watch the clock
And scribble important nothings on blackboards
   (only they're [whiteboards], most of them)
And sometimes
I meet a teacher.

Source: Moss, T., 1969, p. 189. Used with permission.

What Administrators Can Do to Help Students Develop Positive Relationships with Teachers

Administrators' key role is to expect student-educator relationships to build and to show that they value such relationships. That means more than simply telling teachers to do it. Teachers probably need professional development seminars to help them adjust attitudes and get ideas for establishing these bonds with their students. Remember that this idea most likely was not a part of their teacher preparation program. We are asking teachers to have a paradigm shift from viewing themselves as dispensers of information to viewing themselves as mentors. Just as students must learn new skills, so must teachers. In order to do this, they need time, tools, and support. In addition, administrators must work hard to bring parents on board. School policy about home connections needs to be emphasized and understood by all the stakeholders.

1　Administrators can make the school welcoming to parents of diverse backgrounds. They should provide literature in languages spoken in students' homes. It might be a good idea to find someone who can be a translator when needed. Administrators can learn about and show appreciation for the cultures represented in their school. Not all cultures value the same kind of parental involvement in schools. It's important to adapt a school's programs and policies to reflect that understanding.

2　Administrators can provide a place for parents to learn. Many schools provide a family resource room if building space permits. Administrators and other staff members can stock the room with ideas for parenting, videos and pamphlets about child development, and a list of resources parents may consult. A lending library can be established so that parents who can't or won't come to the school still have access to materials. A list of resources can be sent home with each student.

3　Administrators can show parents that their contributions are valued. They can do this by sending home newsletters and making it easy for teachers to make phone calls to the home. Administrators can let parents know how to contact the school (maybe by putting this information on a refrigerator magnet). Parents should be given ideas on how to contribute to their youngster's education, even if they can't physically show up to the school.

4　Administrators can provide teachers with literature and professional development about establishing and maintaining student and home relationships. The teachers' lounge should be flooded with articles and ideas about building bonds with parents and students. Administrators can hold faculty meetings where teachers can share their ideas and ask questions.

Professional development days can be used for teachers to learn about and design means of closer communications. Administrators should be present at those opportunities and learn along with the teachers.

5 Administrators can research how to manipulate the schedule to provide teachers with time to develop relationships. Teachers need to speak to each other about the progress of their students. They also need time to hold one-on-one conferences with students and to contact the home. Many schools now have flex-time periods to provide this valuable time.

6 Administrators can model collaboration. Teaching and learning are difficult tasks, and no one can go it alone. Administrators and teachers need to work together to build a culture of caring. Students need to perceive that all adults are working together to help them succeed.

What Administrators Can Do to Help Students Develop Positive Peer Relationships

1 Administrators can give all students an opportunity to develop leadership and positive peer relations by offering one of the many service club programs that are available to schools. The Builders Club, Key Club, Future Business Leaders, and a number of vocational clubs are a few that offer specific training for students to work in groups on community or competitive projects.

2 Administrators can provide frequent opportunities for students to work in groups, with adults monitoring their work. The adults should assign group roles such as leader, scribe, information gatherer, and communicator.

3 Administrators can plan and implement culture weeks and events that allow students to understand the different and unique cultures present in the school.

4 Administrators can establish a buddy system for new and incoming students so that no one enters the school feeling alone during their first week. Buddies can either come from volunteers, student council, or the entire student body.

5 Administrators can have at least two teachers or outside consultants do a shadow study of at least two students in each building. The students should be selected at random. The purpose of the study is to assess the students' typical school day. The students selected should have a

regular schedule (no exams or assemblies) and be asked if it is OK for someone to shadow them. The observers log what the class and the student do every five minutes during the entire day. The log should include facts, not opinions. At the same time, the observers should note student relationships in the classrooms, hallways, and cafeteria. At the end of the day, the observers should interview the students and ask the following questions:

- What was the highlight of your day?
- What would you like to change about your day?
- How do you think other students in your classes responded to this day?
- Is there anything else about the day in a life of a student here that I should know?

The observers summarize their data without the students' or teachers' names and present their findings to the staff. This snapshot of a student day can be a great starting point for a faculty discussion about building positive student relationships.

6   Administrators can encourage the counselor to set up small support groups for students who are having difficulty fitting in. These groups are especially effective if held during the student lunch time when students who don't fit in are either left to eat alone or are harassed by other students.

7   Administrators can develop and maintain a student advisory council that meets with administrators and counselors at least once a week to discuss student issues and relationships in the school. A rotating membership ensures that students from all age groups, cultures, and groups are represented.

8   Administrators can select a citizen of the week and post the student's picture and reason for selection in the hallway for all to see.

9   Administrators can encourage teachers to use the activities at the end of each chapter in this book to develop relationships among the students in their classes.

10   Administrators can send two positive notes or e-mails home about every student during the school year and encourage teachers to do so. This helps teachers look for positive behaviors in all students and sets a positive tone for parent interaction. The notes may be about class work or citizenship efforts.

What Parents Can Do to Help Students Develop Positive Relationships

1. Parents can understand that youngsters need caring adults other than themselves. Research from the Search Institute (www.search-institute.org) shows that one of the developmental assets that children need for success is caring relationships with parents *and* other adults. Parents need to seek out and rely on trustworthy adults who care about their kids.

2. Parents can provide invaluable information about their children's strengths, challenges, needs, and interests. Parents should talk with teachers and share information about their youngsters, but parents and teachers should avoid presenting an us-versus-them mentality. Students should perceive that parents and teachers are conspiring to help kids achieve.

3. Parents can become involved. That doesn't mean that parents need to spend lots of time in the school. Parents can find out how to support school in the home. For example, they can provide a place and time to reinforce schoolwork. They can stay in communication with teachers, look for and expect progress reports, and talk with teachers about their children's changing needs or family circumstances.

Teachers, administrators, and parents may do everything in their power to help vulnerable students in school, but some problems are difficult to assess and confront. Students who are failing, tardy, absent, undisciplined, and unproductive in school may be having serious problems with their peers. Interviewed students often stated that they just didn't fit in with the school culture. This problem is not just a middle or high school problem. It starts early. As one preschool teacher explained, "I have one little girl who is just plain mean to other kids. The other day I heard her say to another girl, 'let's not play with her, she doesn't have the right kind of clothes on.'" Elementary school teachers are concerned about students who no one will play with during recess or are never chosen for team games. *Cipher in the Snow* (Brigham Young University), a classic story (Todhunter, 1982) and film from 1973, illuminates the growing vulnerability of students in the most poignant way possible. In this true story, an ostracized teen dies and a favorite teacher comes to realize that no one knew the boy well enough to help him through difficult times.

Middle and high school students who have no one to eat lunch with or have different beliefs from the norm face an impossible situation. The use of Internet bullying allows the discomfort of school to follow students home. Girls who are ostracized or bullied may talk to a teacher, counselor, or parent, but boys will most likely respond with physical aggression and anger.

Students at this age who withdraw because of peer problems are especially vulnerable to the use of (or increased use of) drugs and alcohol. There are many students, boys in particular, who do not act out and therefore are not recognized as vulnerable until they have quietly withdrawn and dropped out. There are such significant differences in the ways in which girls and boys respond to school that it is worth the time and effort to structure small groups of same sex students to discuss the issues related to student to student acceptance at both the middle and high school levels.

Summary

Relationships matter more than we tend to think they do. The interactions among those in the school can either encourage or discourage a student's attitude and behavior. All people in the school need to feel that they matter, that they belong, that their work and attendance make a difference, and that someone will miss them if they go away mentally or physically. As class sizes grow, relationships with individual students can suffer. Therefore, we need to build mechanisms that allow students and educators to interact in various and meaningful ways. Students must see clear demonstrations that someone cares and wants to listen. It is only through such human interaction that some students will open themselves up to learning. Too many of our at-risk youth do not trust adults or the educational system. It is only through meaningful and trusting relationships that we can help to break down the walls that some students have built around themselves for defense and self-preservation.

References and Resources

Baumrind, D. (1971). Current patterns of parental authority. *Developmental Psychology Monograph* (No.1 Part 2).

Bergmann, S., Brough, J. and Shepard, D. (2008). *Teach my kid, I dare you: The educator's essential guide to parent involvement.* Larchmont, NY: Eye On Education.

Brough, J., Bergmann, S., and Holt, L. (2006). *Teach me, I dare you!* Larchmont, NY: Eye On Education.

Gurian, M. and Stevens, K. (2005) *The minds of boys.* San Francisco, CA: Jossey-Bass.

Marzano. R. (2003). *Classroom management that works.* Alexandria, VA: ASCD.

Maslow, A. (1954). *Motivation and personality.* New York: Harper.

McCombs, B. L. and Pope, J. E. (1994). *Motivating hard to reach students.* Washington, DC: American Psychological Association, pp. 17–18.

Moss, T. (1969). *Middle school.* Boston, MA: Houghton Mifflin, p. 189.

National Mentoring Partnership, <www.mentoring.org>

RELATIONSHIPS

Search Institute. (October 2003). *Insights and Evidence,* 1 (1). Minneapolis, MN: Search Institute, Retrieved January 8, 2001, from <www.search-institute. org/research/education>

Todhunter, J. M. (1982). *Cipher in the snow.* Provo, UT: KenningHouse.

Vygotsky, L. (1978). *Mind in society: the development of higher psychological processes.* Cambridge, MA: Harvard University Press.

Strategies, Lessons, and Activities for Helping Students Develop Positive RELATIONSHIPS

Valuing Student Feedback

Directions: Allow students to give feedback to teachers. Duplicate questions such as these for students to submit to individual teachers.

On a scale of 1 to 5, with 1 being poor and 5 being excellent, place an X on the line to rate your teacher's ability to help you learn.

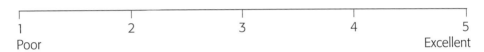

On a scale of 1 to 5, with 1 being poor and 5 being excellent, place an X on the line to rate how well your teacher listens to you.

Please think about the following questions carefully and answer as specifically and clearly as you can:

- What can I do to help you be successful in school?
- How do you think I could improve my teaching skills?

Add your own questions and/or change the other questions on this page to suit your particular needs.

Finding Out About Your Students

Directions: Provide a tape recorder so that students with language or writing difficulties can share their answers and opinions. Use questions or sentence starters like these at the beginning of a new school year or term to determine students' interests and concerns.

Questions

1. What are you interested in? _____

    _____

    _____

2. What are you good at learning or doing? _____

    _____

    _____

3. What is important to you? _____

    _____

    _____

4. What do you want to do in the future? _____

    _____

    _____

5. What do you expect from school? _____

    _____

    _____

6. What do you need help with? _____

    _____

    _____

7. What is your favorite part of the school day? Why? _____

    _____

    _____

8. What would you like to learn about? _____

_____

_____

9. Add your own questions, or change these to suit your needs. _____

_____

_____

Sentence Starters

1. I wish I knew more about _____

_____

2. I wonder why _____

_____

3. I like it when _____

_____

4. I enjoy learning about _____

_____

5. I learn best when _____

_____

6. I have trouble with _____

_____

7. School could be a better place if _____

_____

8. Add your own sentence starters, or change these to suit your needs.

_____

Individual Crisis Intervention and De-Escalation Model

Directions: Use this strategy to help students work through anger issues.

1. Immediately "ACT"

   Attend: Make contact with the student by voice, note, or eyes.

   Calm: Use your voice to reassure them that you will help them. Take them away from the current environment to a quiet, safe, place.

   Treat: Say, "I understand that you are (troubled, angry, upset)." Would you like to tell me or someone else what is troubling you?" or "Do you need the assistance of a doctor or nurse?"

2. Respond to the student.

3. Actively listen to the student's response.

4. Paraphrase what the student said to be sure you understand the message correctly.

5. Ask the student what action he or she needs to take immediately.

6. Ask the student what information he or she needs to make a decision.

7. Answer any questions the student has.

8. Help the student think of a way to solve the problem.

9. Get the student to commit to a positive action.

10. Take the student to the counselor or social worker for further help if necessary. Involve parents if necessary.

11. Provide opportunities for written communication to you from the student.

12. Establish a time the next day for the student to check back with you even if he or she has been to see a counselor or other professional. This continuity of caring is essential to students.

13. Inform the student of possible networks or support systems in the school and community.

Similarities Inventory

Directions: Find a person in the group who shares each of the following characteristics with you.

	Answer	**Name of Person with Similarity**
Birth Month	_____	_____
Favorite Food	_____	_____
Favorite Color	_____	_____
Favorite Movie	_____	_____
Favorite Song	_____	_____

Getting to Know You

Directions: Use this strategy to have students describe themselves or to help students learn about a peer.

Name of Person: _____

What does she or he…

like to think about?

like to talk about?

love?

like to eat?

like to do?

6

Helping Students Develop
RESPECT

"When I approach a child, he inspires in me two sentiments; tenderness for what he is, and respect for what he may become."
Louis Pasteur

"No community can exist without a measure of trust."
Howard Gardner (2006, p. xiv)

What Is Respect?

A meta-analysis of research (Cornelius-White, 2007) concluded that teachers who showed empathy and warmth to their students correlated strongly with higher levels of student participation, motivation, and achievement. A cooperative and positive school and class culture needs to be established in order to provide all students with a safe environment where academic risks can be taken and students can feel free to engage in problem solving and a challenging curriculum. (See Maslow's hierarchy of needs on page 9.) Mutual respect is a key element in such a culture. Respect is the understanding that other people can have different backgrounds, cultures, beliefs, or perspectives, but that doesn't make them wrong. It is the sentiment that one's past does not dictate the future. While trust can be gained slowly among individuals, it cannot be fostered without respect for one another, which can be and should be expected and fostered from day one of the school year. Respect involves abstract abilities to empathize, to listen, and to be open to the perspectives of someone else. It is about granting individuals the benefit of the doubt and giving them a chance to prove themselves worthy. Some students need to be taught these skills, while others have well-developed abilities gained through prior instruction, travel, family background, and rich experiences with others. If trust and respect are established, the dignity of all students and adults can be maintained. Without that dignity, conflicts occur more readily and the emotional, if not physical, safety in the classroom can be diminished. Many at-risk students distrust authority and the school organization. They may buck the system until they learn to respect it. According to Farid (2005), respect is necessary for several reasons:

1. Respect allows people to build trust with others.

2. Respect allows people to build and rebuild relationships.

3. Respect provides people with "an entry" into the other side.

4. Respected members of the community are most likely to be able to bring or encourage peace.

5. Respect can be the key difference in the direction of a conflict.

6. The presence of respect can lead to a positive change

7. Its absence may lead to even more destruction (p. 1).

In order to build trust and respect, all people involved must become aware of shared values, goals, or perspectives. This implies that students and educators need to get to know each other on a personal basis. Communication may not occur serendipitously, so teachers need to plan purposely for it. Teachers can use self-disclosure to create a bond and understanding with students. Time used to foster listening skills, empathy, and perspective-taking (asking for a student's reasoning or point of view) is time well spent. Too often teachers must spend an inordinate amount of time dealing with behavior management issues. Using this time proactively to develop a culture of respect is more efficient than reacting to misbehaviors. Unfortunately, students who have experienced repeated failure may have reached the point where they accept their lot in life. Turning such students around will take time. They may be looking for reasons to distrust their teachers and will try the adults' patience over and over again. Although these students must learn that actions have consequences, teachers will accomplish more by continuing to talk with them and showing respect for their feelings and attitudes than by punishing them. Students need to feel optimism and hope; they need to learn how to behave properly in various situations. They need a caring adult to model respect for them and help them to discover what respect looks and sounds like (see activity on page 137). And if this doesn't occur in the home, then it certainly must occur in the school.

Schools are beset with instances of bullying, teasing, and fighting. A climate of mutual respect and open dialogue is the only way to establish an environment where such destructive behaviors are not tolerated by adults or students. Getting to know people, learning to listen to their ideas, and coming to value their differences, enables growth in valuing their differing opinions and ways of living. According to Lewicki and Tomlinson (2003), trust is necessary for successful conflict resolution. They stated that "...trust is associated with enhanced cooperation, information sharing, and problem solving" (p. 1). Trust evolves into empathy, which allows people to see a situation from someone else's perspective. It helps to remove blame and opens the relationship to meaningful dialogue. Empathy includes the following:

- seeing through the eyes of another

- genuineness and sincerity

- valuing the opinions of another

- giving another the benefit of the doubt

- openness to differing perspectives and lifestyles

- understanding and valuing human differences.

In order to respect others, people must first develop self-respect. Many schools are implementing programs or units of instruction that focus on self-respect, respect for others, and respect for property and the environment.

What Teachers Can Do to Help Students Develop Respect

1 Teachers need to foster relationships so that they get to know their students, the students to know the teacher, and the students to know each other. Ice breakers are essential in the beginning of the relationship to enhance group dynamics and prevent some interaction problems. During the first few days of the school year or semester, teachers can set time aside for get-to-know-you activities. Examples of ice-breaking activities can be found at the following Web sites:

- www.icebreakers.ws

- www.educationworld.com

- www.ion.illinois.edu/institutes/fsi/2005/presentations/3/IceBreak ingActivities.pdf

- www.buzzle.com/articles/fun-ice-breaker-games.html

2 Teachers can recognize that how adults talk with students makes a difference. The distinction is debate versus dialogue. Debate assumes a win or loss; each side believes itself to have the "right" answer. Dialogue assumes that individuals are open to listening to someone else's perspective while contributing their own ideas for consideration. Yankelovich (1999) states that debate is combative and coercive, while dialogue is collaborative. In the latter, participants talk together to reach a common understanding. Dialogue shows respect for someone else's ideas and perspectives. Dialogue implies that people are open to examining their preconceived

RESPECT

notions while debate requires defensiveness against the opinions of others. Listening to the students' ideas fosters communication that allows the teacher to understand the students' plights and reasons for certain behaviors. Phrases such as "Thanks for sharing that idea," "You make a good point," or "I hadn't thought of that before" show the students that teachers are eager to hear their opinions and value their contributions. That being said, students must also realize that giving excuses for certain behaviors is unacceptable. An explanation of problem behaviors does not excuse the behavior. This is an opportunity for teachers to help the student to learn new ways of behaving when presented with similar situations. Short one-on-one conferences with individual students allow teachers to understand more fully the wants and needs of the youngsters. The attention shows caring and garners respect.

3 Teachers should model and teach active listening skills (sometimes called empathic listening skills), which are important for both students and educators. Teachers can use good eye contact and offer nonverbal affirmations like nodding, gestures like a thumbs-up or an okay sign, and verbal cues like "yes, I see" or "uh-huh." Kelly (nd) listed the following steps to teach active listening skills:

- ◆ Suspend other things you are doing, and look at the person.
- ◆ Listen not merely to the words, but also to the feeling content.
- ◆ Be sincerely interested in what the other person is talking about.
- ◆ Restate what the person said.
- ◆ Ask clarification questions once in a while.
- ◆ Be aware of your own feelings and strong opinions.
- ◆ If you have to state your views, say them only after you have listened (p. 2).

Active listening is critical when teachers have to de-escalate a volatile situation. It sends the message that the teachers hear what students are saying, are interested in their explanation or point of view, and are withholding judgment about the situation until all the cards are on the table. When adults show this kind of empathy, they bolster students' confidence and esteem, reduce conflict and stress, allow students to maintain dignity, and build on a trusting relationship, in addition to getting to the pertinent facts about a situation. (See listening activity on page 139.) The number one piece of advice at-risk students offered when interviewed was "listen to me."

4 Teachers can discuss with students those actions that foster respect or disrespect in the classroom. Students can work together to define specific behaviors. Teachers can have the students recall instances when they felt respected or disrespected and how they felt about it. What actions caused those feelings? What would they have preferred? Students might recall a time when they showed respect or disrespect

for someone else. Why did they choose that behavior? Teachers may wish to use *Don't Laugh at Me,* a free multi-age, multi-media program from Operation Respect, an organization founded by Peter Yarrow to foster respect (www.operationrespect.org/curricula/index.php). Using this program, children learn to be sensitive to the feelings of others and become aware of how their actions may impact others. It can involve the class, the school, the home, and the community.

5 Teachers can design units of instruction that help students learn respect for property and the environment. One high school initiated a long-term watershed study of the effects of pollution on the Chesapeake Bay. Students in biology class studied the bay and analyzed water samples while they learned about pollutants and their effect on the environment. Many places, like New York City, have designed watershed studies and even offer grants (see www.nyc.gov/html/dep/html/environmental_education/index.shtml.) Elementary school students can carefully pick up and analyze trash in the school yard and discuss how it denigrates the school environment. Students involved in science fairs can be encouraged to study pollutants and local environmental issues, offering suggestions for improvement.

6 Teachers can teach good citizenship, especially in social studies classes. Many Web sites provide activities for teaching citizenship to all age ranges. Citizenship, which is an abstract term, can be defined and examples given. Students can brainstorm examples and non-examples.

What Administrators Can Do to Help Students Develop Respect

1 The most important role of the administrator is modeling and expecting a culture of respect in the school. Just as teachers are expected to listen to their students, so must the administrator build a mechanism to listen to the building's teachers. Administrators can establish a steering committee that meets regularly to discuss school strengths and challenges. Administrators should make sure that teachers perceive communications to be open and honest.

2 Administrators need to raise awareness of the Search Institute's Developmental Assets (www.search-institute.org) among teachers, parents, and students and should plan with parents and community members to ensure that students are developing these assets. Longitudinal research conducted by the institute shows that children benefit from increased numbers of identified assets that are fostered by the school, the home, the community, and by the students themselves. Forty assets, listed by age range, are grouped into the categories of support, empowerment,

boundaries and expectations, constructive use of time, commitment to learning, positive values, social competencies, and positive identity. In Adams County, PA, a group of educators and community members hold annual leadership conferences for all the seventh-graders in the county (one for girls and one for boys). Using the assets in a pre- and post-assessment framework, these adults, in conjunction with middle-school students, choose topics and speakers that will appeal to young adolescents and foster their growth. Popular topics include manners, dealing with stress, respecting each other, health and nutrition, bully-ing, and peer pressure. Students involved report increased achievement in the developmental assets and a perception that the adults in the com-munity care about their welfare. School counselors are the backbone of this initiative, which is coordinated by the school districts, community hospital, Girl Scouts, the American Association of University Women, and Gettysburg College. Local school administrators support this event and provide bus transportation to the conference and planning time for the school counselors. (Contact jbrough@comcast.net or johnwag-ner1949@gmail.com for further information.)

3 Administrators must pay attention to the school environment. They need to recognize that the school's physical environment may have a significant impact on children's health and safety, and find resources like the Illinois Environmental Protection Agency (www.epa.state.il.us/p2/green-schools) that have developed programs designed to improve the ability of schools to provide a safe and healthy environment. The EPA also offers environmental-education programs for use in schools. (See www.epa.gov/enviroed or the EPA of individual states, like California at www.calepa.ca.gov/education.) The school environment should be one that makes students feel secure and respected. One school has no doors on the bathroom stalls. Some students report that they won't use these bathrooms because of the lack of privacy. These same students state that they don't care about the school and wouldn't think twice about scrawling graffiti on its walls. Obviously, the students feel disre-spected and, in turn, show their disrespect for the building.

What Parents Can Do to Help Students Develop Respect

Parents have the most influence on the degree of respect their children learn. They can model respectful relationships and discuss appropriate behaviors with their children. Children are never too young or too old to learn about respect.

1. Parents can expect cooperation and respect in the home.
2. Parents can teach children that their actions may impact others.

3. Parents can encourage young children to share their toys.

4. Parents can encourage older children to mentor younger ones in the family.

5. Parents can help their children learn the value of telling the truth.

6. One of the best ways parents can teach respect (and foster reading skills) is to use children's literature to initiate discussion about the topic of respect, sharing, and getting along with others. Some recommended books are listed at the end of this chapter.

Silverman (2008) offers the following ten tips to parents who are trying to teach respect and eliminate disrespect:

1. model

2. expect (have high expectations)

3. teach

4. praise

5. discuss

6. correct

7. acknowledge

8. understand

9. reinforce

10. reward

Summary

It is difficult to trust someone who has more authority and seems unapproachable. People in power and control make decisions that others are not always privy to. Educators must ask themselves how to get students to follow direction when they've trusted someone in the past and have gotten burned for it. A sense of trust is built over time as relationships are tested and grow (see Chapter 5 on relationships), but respect can be given and modeled from day one. Try giving all students the benefit of the doubt—regardless of their past behaviors, mistakes, or circumstances. Let them start fresh every day. Many students told the authors that they behaved badly in some circumstances, because that was the only choice they saw that they had at the time. Instead of merely meting out punishment, help the students to learn alternatives. Instead of blaming, have a dialogue that shows not only that adults care, but that teachers have faith in them to do the right thing. Listen to their point of view. Talk with them kindly. Certainly students must be informed when they've done something wrong, but teachers need to show the belief that students can learn and change their behaviors. Remember that adults make mistakes, too, and need to admit it. One of this book's authors blamed a student in her class for giving a flip answer in class, which disrupted the flow of the lesson and caused the entire class to get off task. Fully ready to read the riot act to this student, she asked why he had made such a ridiculous comment. His answer showed that his response wasn't flippant at all. He was merely explaining his thought processes, which were quite different from the teacher's. The teacher had to apologize and admit that she had misread the intent of the student's comment.

Understand that many students' poor attitudes and behaviors have resulted from years of bad experiences and failures. Comments are often made without thinking. Motivation can be learned. Proper behavior can be learned. But the learning will occur only when the students sense a safe environment in which to try out new behaviors and attitudes.

References and Resources

References

Cornelius-White, J. (2007). Learner-centered teacher-student relationships are effective: A meta-analysis, *Review of Educational Research* 77(1), 113–143.

Farid, S. (July 2005). "Respect." *Beyond Intractability*, G. Burgess and H. Burgess (Eds.), Conflict Research Consortium, University of Colorado, Boulder. Retrieved from <www.beyondintractability.org/essay/respect>.

Gardner, H. (2006). *Changing Minds: The Act and Science of Changing Our Own and Other People's Minds*. Boston, MA: Harvard Business School Press.

Kelly, M. (nd). Active listening for the classroom: An important motivational strategy. About.com. Retrieved January 28, 2011, from <http://712educators.about.com/cs/activelistening/a/activelistening_2.htm>

Lewicki, R. J. and Tomlinson, E. C. (December 2003). Trust and trust building. *Beyond Intractability*. G. Burgess and H. Burgess (Eds.), Conflict Research Consortium, University of Colorado. Retrieved from <www.beyondintractability.org/essay/trust_building>

Operation Respect. http://www.operationrespect.org

Silverman, R. (April 12, 2008). 10 tips on teaching respect to children: you can't get it if you don't give it. Retrieved from <www.drrobynsilverman.com/parenting-tips/10-tips-on-teaching-respect-to-children-you-cant-get-it-if-you-dont-give-it>

Yankelovich, D. (1999). *The magic of dialogue: transforming conflict into cooperation*. New York, NY: Simon & Schuster.

Resources: Books with a Message About Respect

Crossing Jordan, Adrian Fogelin: black-white relations, Grades 5–8

Star Girl, Jerry Spinelli: being different and accepting oneself, Grades 6 and above

Some Kids Are Deaf, Lola M. Schaefer

Some Kids Use Wheelchairs, Lola M. Schaefer

Keith Edward's Different Day, Karin Melberg Schwier: Keith encounters people who seem different as he goes through his day.

Don't Laugh At Me, Steve Seskin and Allen Shamblin: A children's book on bullying; includes music, lyrics, and a CD.

Toby!: Toby's Flying Lesson (1st Edition), Cindy Szekeres: Toby the mouse and Bob the bird discover that even though they can't do the same things (fly and romp), by working together they can use their abilities to do something they both enjoy.

Different Just Like Me, Lori Mitchell: A young girl meets many different people and, like the flowers in her grandmother's garden, learns to appreciate the beauty of individual differences.

Not Better, Not Worse, Just Different, Sharon Scott: A book to help children to be kind to one another and accepting of the differences between people.

Understanding Human Differences: Multicultural Education for a Diverse America (with MyEducationLab) (3rd Edition), Kent Koppelman and Lee Goodhart

I'm Like You, You're Like Me: A Child's Book About Understanding and Celebrating Each Other, Cindy Gainer

Come Over To My House, Dr. Seuss: Young children learn about how different people live.

Celebrating Differences Globally: Ernst Interactive Media (EIM) invites you to "bring children from each continent into your elementary classroom" through the Hello! From Around the World! video series. The extensive collection of countries and regions represented includes: Bali, Japan, Ecuador, Venezuela, Central Europe, Egypt, Australia, South Pacific Islands, Mexico, Central America, and the United States.

Reach Out and Give (part of the "Learning to Get Along Series), Cheri Meiners: A book for young children about sharing.

RESPECT

Strategies, Lessons, and Activities for Helping Students Develop RESPECT

Reaction Reflection

Ask students to consider the following events. How would they or others react to the situations?

1. Someone trips and falls down a set of stairs.

2. Someone drops all of their books and papers.

3. Someone gets sick and throws up in class.

4. Someone with a speech impediment, like a lisp or stutter, tries to read aloud in class.

Ask students "How would you feel if it were you? How would you *like* others to react? Why?"

Reacting to Others' Misfortunes

Show clips from *America's Funniest Home Videos*. Ask, "Why do people laugh at someone else's mistake or misfortune? What are the alternatives?"

T-Chart Defining Respect

Directions: Fill in the following T-chart.

Respect

What it looks like	What it sounds like

Respect Map

Directions: On each line, write a word that is a synonym of respect, is an example of respect, or that defines respect.

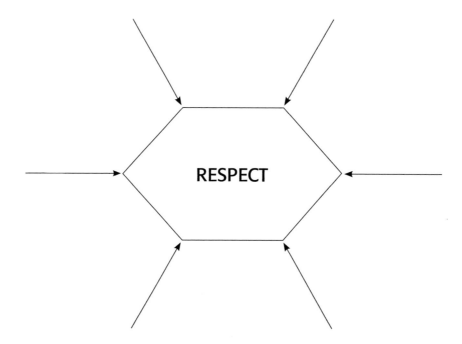

RESPECT

Listening Triad

Step 1: Divide students into groups of three.

Step 2: Have one student talk about the assigned topic for one minute while another listens, and the third evaluates the listener's response. The students should not take notes but practice listening. The evaluator should look for the following behaviors:

- accurate reiteration of what the speaker said
- completeness of the statements
- eye contact
- non-judgmental comments

Step 3: Then, have students shift roles until all three students experience each of the roles.

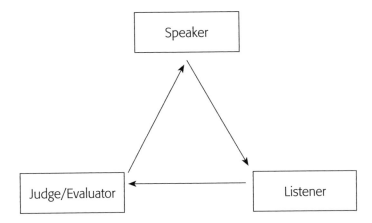

7

Helping Students Develop
READING SKILLS

"There are many little ways to enlarge your child's world. Love of books is the best of all."

Jacqueline Kennedy

What Challenges Do Struggling Readers Face?

Of the people with the lowest literacy skills, 43 percent live in poverty, 17 percent receive food stamps, and 70 percent have no job or a part-time job. The cost of illiteracy to businesses and taxpayers is estimated at $20 billion annually (National Institute for Literacy, p. 2). Reading matters. Everyone knows it, but finds it difficult to help challenged readers, who often not only don't read well, but also frequently don't want to read at all. Many perceive themselves as hopeless readers. The coping mechanisms they develop become barriers between themselves and any kind of reading ("Reading sucks" is a common statement among poor readers. Sorry for being blunt, but that's exactly what many of them say). Challenged readers say they don't like to read or don't want to read instead of acknowledging their difficulty understanding the text; they lack confidence in their abilities to make sense of the reading. Giving them reading assignments for homework is futile. Few kids will read the material, and many who do can't understand it. What's a teacher to do? Fortunately, there are sufficient research and strategies to help struggling readers.

What Teachers Can Do to
Help Students Develop Reading Skills

1 Recognize that students need skills in identifying words and skills in comprehension, including vocabulary building and reading fluency. What many struggling readers don't realize is that successful reading involves thinking. Reading is more than simply decoding the words. Surely you have heard students accurately decode words aloud in a text without any understanding. They read individual words, one at a time, without fluency to string the words together into ideas (they've got the words, but they ain't got the tune). Because they are concentrating solely on word identification, they lose fluency and meaning. Many devices have been invented to help students to apply this important comprehension skill.

- ◆ Model reading fluency
- ◆ Read silently before reading aloud
- ◆ Use tape recorders so kids can hear themselves read
- ◆ Use buddy reading
- ◆ Help kids to chunk the reading so they begin to read phrases as opposed to single words.

2 Students must learn how to interact with a text in a way that involves their thinking. Employ the three phases of cognitive processing for reading: the pre-active stage where students get ready to read by accessing prior knowledge and becoming familiar with the text to be read; the interactive stage where students are reading and thinking about what they are reading by connecting to prior knowledge, asking themselves questions, and checking for their understanding; and the reflective phase where they summarize what they have read and make decisions about its meaning. The following questions can help students with each phase of processing:

Skim: Look at the book's cover and illustrations and read the first and last pages.

Predict _____ What do you think this book will be about?

Read _____ Read a few pages

Check _____ Did your prediction come true?

Predict again _____ What do you think will happen next?

Read _____ Read several more pages

Do you want to change your prediction? Why or why not?

Check for understanding. What is happening?

When you are done reading:

Summarize _____ Name the who or what.

_____ Tell the most important thing about the who or what.

_____ State the main idea in 10 words or less.

3　Building confidence in students' reading abilities has to be the teacher's first priority. Begin by focusing on students' motivation to read. Start with a reading history (Tovani, 2000). Ask them to think about a book, poem, or magazine article that has had an impact on them—either positively or negatively (many will need to remember back to their days as toddlers). Have them recall why this selection was important to them (Tovani, 2000, p. 10). Some kids will fondly remember books read to them as preschoolers. Many struggling readers have lost that sense of wonder that books can impart. The loss is often a result of embarrassment at one's struggle to read and the lack of confidence in reading ability. The first step is to recapture some of that magic that a good book can bring. Reading classic books for children can spark fond memories in older youngsters. Children's books can be useful in teaching the various content areas, too. For example, using various versions of *The Three Little Pigs* can help students compare and contrast; draw conclusions, discover morals of a story, see how using different vocabulary can change the tone of a text; or learn how illustrations help to deliver a message. All these skills, and more, can be taught using non-threatening text. We can spark motivation with these ideas:

- ◆ Choice in reading material and learning tasks with a wide range of choices provided
- ◆ Provision of texts that appeal to both genders and youth from diverse backgrounds and with various interests
- ◆ Selection of appropriate difficulty of reading material and assignments
- ◆ Modeling of reading and writing strategies
- ◆ Guided practice
- ◆ Use of visuals like graphic organizers or semantic maps
- ◆ Use of movies and audio tapes
- ◆ Buddy reading
- ◆ A purpose is given for every reading assignment
- ◆ Use of music, drama, and art
- ◆ Teacher read-alouds and literature discussions
- ◆ Consideration of students' background knowledge

4 Teachers need to find out what interests their students and provide books that spark that their interest. On page 113 is a vignette about a student teacher who sparks a ninth-grade boy's interest in literature by sharing with him magazine articles and information about the Chevy Camaro. In a content area, teachers can find out what the students want to learn about in the unit and let them choose topics to read about themselves. Teachers can actively solicit students' interests by talking with them one-on-one and by giving them an interest inventory to submit. Inventory questions and sentence starters may include the following:

- What do you wish you could learn about?
- What hobbies and interests do you have?
- What are your strengths?
- I wish I knew…
- I wonder about…
- I enjoy…

5 The teachers' third step is to guide students to recall prior knowledge to provide a hook that will help them relate to what they are reading. The SQ3R strategy (**S**urvey the chapter, ask yourself **Q**uestions to be answered during reading, **R**ead, **R**ecite what you've read, and **R**eview) is one method of summoning prior knowledge. Students write down questions they hope to have answered in the reading. Another effective strategy is KWL (What we **K**now, what we **W**ant to found out about, what we have **L**earned), or KWHL, which includes *How we will find out* as the third step. Kids often don't know what to look for or pay attention to in their reading, and their comprehension suffers. When students have a purpose that helps them understand why they are reading, they can focus on pertinent information instead of paying attention to irrelevant ideas. The purpose should help them identify what to look for, what to pay attention to. A Reading Road Map can help students pay attention to the right information or ideas. (See www.middleweb.com/ReadWrkshp/RWdownld/Roadmap.pdf for an example.) Students learn best when they attach new information to previous knowledge. Gathering background information can be done in many different ways, but it is a step we tend to omit. Reflecting on prior knowledge may remind students of key vocabulary and help them to identify questions that can become the focus for the new learning. Without that focus, many students have trouble determining the main idea or gathering pertinent information. Students need to get ready to read before diving in. They need to prepare by making predictions, skimming the reading and its illustrations, defining a purpose, and learning new vocabulary.

6 Teachers can identify students' abilities and scaffold instruction to increasingly challenging levels, which will also help build students' self-confidence as readers. Frequent formal and informal nonthreatening assessments before, during, and after instruction provide teachers with data to design instruction at the proper level by identifying skills the students need to work on. Specific skills groups can then be designed to focus of the particular skills needed. The assessments also show the students evidence of their progress. At-risk students who were interviewed complained that they were repeatedly given work that was too easy or too repetitive, or tasks that they had already completed successfully. Once instruction begins, students should receive concrete feedback at regular intervals. Students need to know that their efforts matter and that they are being successful and making academic strides, regardless of how small that success may be. Student-designed goals and student self-evaluation also help struggling students gain control over their own learning. To help struggling readers, teachers can try the following strategies identified by Pearson, Roehler, Dole and Duffy (1992) that are often used by good readers:

- Use existing knowledge to make sense of text.
- Ask questions before, during, and after reading.
- Draw inferences.
- Monitor comprehension. (Am I understanding what I read?)
- Use strategies when comprehension breaks down.
- Make decisions about what is important.
- Synthesize information to create new thinking.

Successful reading demands that readers check for their own understanding and learn ways to adjust when they are confused. When students learn the steps listed above, they gain abilities to monitor their own reading, which leads them to independent reading.

7 Teachers can teach fluency skills. Reading is more than decoding words. Students may accurately decode words without understanding what they are reading. They read individual words but don't have the fluency to string the words together into ideas (again, they've got the words, but they ain't got the tune). By concentrating solely on word identification, they lose the overall meaning.

Rasinki (2004) has written quite a bit of helpful information regarding the importance of and strategies to teach reading fluency. He stresses the use of repeated readings to guide students to fluency and encourages assisted reading, where students practice their reading skills with a more accomplished reader. While listening to good readers read is certainly a critical first step, fluency is taught purposefully through guided steps and repetition. Wolf and Katzir-Cohen (2001) agree, explaining that fluency is a skill often neglected. Sometimes we just expect youngsters to develop fluent reading without teaching them to do so. Certainly fluency does come naturally to some students as they learn to read. But others, haunted by word decoding, meaning, and other comprehension skills, struggle to make words flow in a way that makes sense. Fluency is not just reading fast, it is reading with flow in a way that allows comprehension. Some helpful ideas include the following strategies:

- fluency assessments
- buddy reading, assisted reading, side-by-side reading
- repeated readings of familiar text: students gradually expand
- modeled reading (students listen to a good reader read) followed by taped reading (students listen to a tape of their own reading and reflect on the difference)
- chunked reading of phrases as opposed to single words
- silent reading: students read silently before reading aloud
- self-selected goals for fluency improvement
- rhythm, rhyme, poetry, and music.

A helpful fluency rubric Rasinki created can be found at http://www.timrasinski.com/presentations/multidimensional_fluency_rubric_4_factors.pdf. Many of Rasinki's presentations, strategies, and helpful hints can be accessed at his Web site at www.timrasinski.com/?page=presentations. Wolf's work can be found at the Scholastic site www2.scholastic.com/browse/article.jsp?id=4466

8 | Teachers can teach vocabulary-building and concept development skills. Youngsters who have a larger working vocabulary tend to be better readers. They are not as often stumped when encountering new words. To build a student's bank of vocabulary, teachers should use a wide range of strategies that appeal to various learning styles. Simply looking a word up in the dictionary and copying down a definition does not lead to ease of use of the new words. Readers tend to learn vocabulary when they make connections between known and unknown words. Teachers can try these examples of vocabulary-building and concept development activities:

- Link new words to something kids are already familiar with.
- Have kids brainstorm synonyms or words that connect to new words.
- Find non-examples of the words. What doesn't fit? What is the opposite?
- Use visuals created by the students (see page 154).
- Use words in context rather than in isolation, for example, "a mouse nibbled on the cheese" provides clues to the meaning of *nibbled*.

- ◆ Make a web or semantic map of new concepts and how they relate to previously known words and concepts. Understanding the connection is important.
- ◆ Use comparison and contrast.
- ◆ Use new terms frequently.
- ◆ Use affixes and their meanings.

9 | Teachers can solicit help. They can't do it alone. Some classes are so big that teachers can't get to every student. Teachers might wish to find partners who can help. They can go to senior centers and to local United Way and Adult Literacy programs. Many retired teachers would enjoy becoming a literacy coach at a school. Many of these volunteers need minimal training since they may have been reading instructors themselves. A local college's education department might also be helpful. All college students enrolled in teacher preparation programs are required to work in schools prior to their student teaching experience. Teachers can get those future teachers into their classrooms on a regular basis. It's a win-win situation. When adults in the family get literacy support, their children benefit as well. Some schools set up evening literacy programs in the school library. Kids come to the sessions with their parents. While mom and dad are improving their reading skills, their youngsters can be completing homework, reading, or doing research. Often, teachers take turns attending these evening classes to act as resources for the children who need extra help or support. Through such programs, kids perceive their parents as viewing reading as important. Such a perception goes a long way in sparking motivation and interest for the child.

10 | Teachers can find mentors for their most vulnerable students. A mentor can act as an advocate for at-risk students, communicating with families and educators for the child's benefit. The mentor can encourage school participation, check on student absences and tardies, and goad parents into supporting their children's educations at home. A mentor can be a listener and can spend time with a child reading.

What Administrators Can Do to Help Students Develop Reading Skills

In order to be successful in supporting our struggling learners, including those with learning disabilities, educators must be intentional and rigorous in their efforts. Trying something now and then won't work. Trying out random ideas won't either. Response to Intervention (RtI) was developed to make sure that no students fall through the cracks. It is a deliberate three-tiered plan to identify students at risk, assess and meet their individual needs on a planned and timely basis, and evaluate the success of interventions. RtI isn't done alone in a classroom with the door closed. Stakeholders gather resources, identify a review of research-based effective strategies, and carefully construct a plan. School personnel and families are integrally involved. The classroom becomes one of meeting individual student needs rather than one where the teacher directs the whole class as one. RtI seeks the answers to the following questions:

1. What is/are the *specific* problem(s)?

2. Why does it/they exist?

3. What are the student's strengths and weaknesses?

4. What should be done to ameliorate the problem(s)? What are the *specific* goals? How long should the intervention last?

5. Is the plan working? How do we know? What do we know? What is the student's specific response to the specific intervention? What assessments will we use to determine the answers to these questions?

6. Where do we go from here?

Assessment is the cornerstone of RtI. The effective school develops specific means of identifying students at risk as well as their particular academic challenges. Carefully planned lessons are then used with students either individually or in small skills groups. Formal and informal assessments keep track of the students' progress on a regular basis and instruction is adapted accordingly. The data collected from these assessments are analyzed carefully, and changes are made in the student's instruction when warranted. *No student continues with ineffective programs or instructional strategies.* Well-implemented RtI models put an end to students languishing in remedial classes focused on whole-group instruction using drill-and-kill worksheets. Rather, if a student fails to make progress, instruction is changed accordingly. Instructional modifications become the norm rather than the exception. The RtI model has three tiers of instruction:

Tier 1: Students receive high-quality, scientifically based instruction that meets their individual needs. Students are screened regularly to identify struggling learners who need additional support.

Tier 2: Students are given increasingly intensive instruction on the basis of levels of performance and rates of progress.

Tier 3: Students are given individualized instruction in needed skills and measures to prevent other areas of struggle are identified and used. (See http://www.rtinetwork.org/essential/tieredinstruction/tier3/considering tier3 for more information.)

Response to Intervention models can be used for all students with academic or behavioral challenges. Educators are encouraged to identify research-based effective strategies to address specific student needs. Faculty meeting and planning time is used to stay on top of the literature and monitor the progress of struggling students. The individual attention to specific needs pays off by preventing further problems and showing youngsters concretely that they can achieve.

What Parents Can Do to Help Students Develop Reading Skills

Nothing affects academic success like reading does. It is essential that children sense that their parents view reading as pleasurable and important (whether or not that appreciation for reading is accurate). Parents need to provide lots of quality reading material for their youngsters from the time they are infants. If money is an issue to providing quality reading material, then the town library should be used on a *regular basis* and parents should contact the school librarian for recommendations of good books for their children. Parents can read aloud to their children, share the reading, and model reading for pleasure and information. Reading has to be evident every day in the home. If parents are illiterate, they should not only use the library, they should also join an adult literacy program and learn to read along with their children.

Summary

Many at-risk youngsters perceive themselves as incapable of being good students, so why bother. Much of that perception stems from an inability to read effectively and efficiently. For many, reading isn't a labor of love; it's just plain labor. By the middle grades, many students have given up on themselves as readers, and many teachers have given up on these students. These kids *can* learn to read well. We just need to realize that they need more help in understanding words and building fluency. All educators need to see themselves as teachers of reading. Educators need to determine students' strengths and use these skills and interests to scaffold vocabulary development. Students need time to practice their fluency in a safe place, where others can't taunt them and roll their eyes at the stilted flow and pronunciations. Let students hear good readers read while they follow along. Talk openly about what a passage means and how you figured it out. Use both student and teacher think-alouds to demonstrate thought processes and assess student misunderstandings. Such strategies not only help with reading skills, they also help students to understand more thoroughly the information being discussed. Choose some motivating selections to read. Match them with student interests. Help them to get excited to read and show them concretely that they're making improvements in their reading skills.

References and Resources

References

Baker, S. K., Simmons, D. C., & Kame'enui, E. J. (1995). *Vocabulary acquisition: Curricular and instructional implications for diverse learners.* (Tech. Rep. No. 14). Eugene, OR: University of Oregon, National Center to Improve the Tools of Educators.

Dickson, S. V., Simmons, D. C., & Kame'enui, E. J. (1995). *Text organization and its relation to reading comprehension: A synthesis of the research.* National Center to Improve the Tools of Educators. [Online]. Available: http://idea.uoregon.edu/~ncite/documents/techrep/tech17.html

Marzano, R., Pickering, D., and Pollock, J. (2001). *Classroom instruction that works: Research-based strategies for increasing student achievement.* Alexandria, VA: ASCD.

Mastropieri, M. A. & Scruggs, T. E. (2000). *The inclusive classroom: Strategies for effective instruction.* Upper Saddle River, NJ: Merrill Prentice-Hall.

National Institute for Literacy (2007). The National Illiteracy Action Project 2007–2012. Retrieved from www.talkingpage.org/NIAP2007.pdf.

Pearson, P. D., Roehler, L. R., Dole, J. A. & Duffy, G. G. (1992). Developing expertise in reading comprehension. In J. Samuels and A. Farstrup (Eds.), *What Research Has to Say About Reading Instruction* (2nd ed., pp. 145–199). Newark, DE: International Reading Association.

Rasinski, T. (March 2004). Creating fluent readers. *Educational Leadership*, 61(6), 46–51.

See also Rasinki's fluency rubric at http://www.timrasinski.com/presentations/multidimensional_fluency_rubric_4_factors.pdf

Rasinki's other work can be found at http://www.timrasinski.com/?page=presentations

Response to Intervention Network. http://www.rtinetwork.org/?gclid=CJGX14G-3qgCFcU65QodOUlS0Q

Tovani, C. (2000). *I Read It, But I Don't Get It: Comprehension Strategies for Adolescent Readers.* Portland, ME: Stenhouse.

United States Department of Education (Winter, 2001). Lifelong learning: National adult literacy survey,. *Education Statistics Quarterly* (Vol. 3, Issue 4).

University of Kansas Center for Research on Learning. *Strategic Instruction Model.* Retrieved January 20, 2011 from http://www.kucrl.org/sim/index.shtml

Wolf, M. & Katzir-Cohen, T. (2001). Reading fluency and its intervention. *Scientific Studies of Reading.* (Special Issue on Fluency). (Eds.E. Kameenui & D. Simmons). 5, p. 211–238.

Resources

http://www.rtinetwork.org—The RTI Action Network is a program of the National Center for Learning Disabilities, funded by the Cisco Foundation

http://www.rti4success.org—National Center On Response to Intervention.

http://www.nasponline.org/resources/handouts/rtiprimer.pdf— resource for involving parents from the National Association of School Psychologists.

http://www.ldonline—information about learning disabilities, including ADHD, and RtI

http://www.jimwrightonline.com/php/rti/rti_wire.php—links to Internet resources

http://www.interventioncentral.org/—free information and downloads with some teaching tips.

http://www.timrasinski.com—lots of information from a well-known reading researcher

Graphic Organizers and Visual Representations:

http://www.edhelper.com/teachers/General_graphic_organizers.htm

http://www.edhelper.com/teachers/General_graphic_organizers.htm http://t4.jordan.k12.ut.us/teacher_resources/inspiration_templates— templates for several different kinds of visual representatives of vocabulary and concepts.

http://www.ncrel.org/sdrs/areas/issues/students/learning/lr1grorg. htm—graphic organizers from NCREL (North Central Regional Educational Laboratory 1988).

http://www.eduplace.com/graphicorganizer/index.jsp—lots of graphic organizers

http://www.everythingesl.net/inservices/graphic_organizers.php— graphic organizers from EverythingESL—good for use by students for whom English is a second language.

Strategies, Lessons, and Activities to
Help Students Develop
READING SKILLS

Vocabulary and Concept-Building Activities

Content Enhancement Routines

These ideas will help students to learn and broaden their vocabulary and concept base through various perspectives and learning styles.
www.kucrl.org/sim/content.shtml

Comparison Routine

The comparison routine requires the students to complete a table, which analyzes the similarities and differences between two or more concepts. Dickson, Simmons, & Kameenui (1995) identified the following steps for helping students to compare and contrast concepts in secondary textbooks:

1. Identify two topics being compared and contrasted.

2. Look for key compare/contrast words such as *alike*, *different*, or *but*.

3. Determine organization of the compare/contrast structure. This can be:
   - Whole/whole, where the author describes the topics separately, with a different paragraph or set of paragraphs for each.
   - Part/part, where the author presents a feature-by-feature comparison of two topics.
   - Mixed, where the author might first discuss each topic separately, and then in another paragraph provide a feature-by-feature analysis.

4. Locate the explanation of how the topics are the same.

5. Locate the explanation of how the topics are different.

Examples, Non-Examples (version 1)

When encountering a new concept, students can list examples in one column, then non-examples in another column. For example:

Continents

examples	non-examples
Australia	Canada
North America	England
Europe	Japan

Examples, Non-Examples (version 2)

In the following list of terms, students can cross out the word that doesn't fit and add one that does.

democracy

dictatorship

congress

monarchy

oligarchy

Your word: _____

Advance Organizers

An advance organizer helps students to understand what to focus on and what to expect. It helps them to tap into prior knowledge and organize their thoughts and actions for instruction. Put the agenda on the board or overhead. Outline the purpose of the reading and define the "look-fors." Look for ideas at the Web site http://www.netnet.org/instructors/design/goalsobjectives/advance.htm

Context Clues

Teach students these five kinds of context clues and examples, and have them search for their own examples as they read.

Type of Context Clue	Word Example	Use Example
synonym	mutiny	This mutiny was an unexpected rebellion.
punctuation definition	photosynthesis	Photosynthesis: the process by which green plants make food
experience/ familiarity	nibble	The little mouse nibbled on the wedge of cheese.
comparison/ contrast	frugal	Although usually frugal, the man went on a spending spree.
examples	primates	We saw primates such as apes, chimpanzees, monkeys, and orangutans.

Critical Attributes

Students define the word, list any characteristics and synonyms for it, describe it in detail, then, if possible, draw a visual representation of the word.

Isthmus: a narrow strip

connects 2 larger bodies

could be land or strip of tissue in the body

Example: Panama

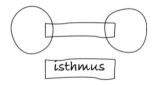

isthmus

Multiple Meaning Clues

New Word	Example	Non-Example	Clue	Visual
mutiny	uprising dissatisfaction disobeying rebellion	obeying following orders trusting the leader	*Mutiny on the Bounty*	Walk the plank, Captain!

New Word	Example	Non-Example	Clue	Visual
autobiography	Book about myself	Fiction Story about someone else	Auto = self Bio = life graph = writing	My Life By Rhoda Book

Story Character Description

Provide a worksheet like this for students to use during or after reading a story. You can change the questions to suit the character and book.

What was s/he thinking?

What did s/he believe in?

What was s/he doing?

How did s/he feel?

What 3 adjectives would describe him/her?

1.

2.

3.

What was s/he like?

Name of Character: _____

Visual Story Mapping

Provide a worksheet like this for students to use during or after reading a story. You can change the questions to suit the character and book.

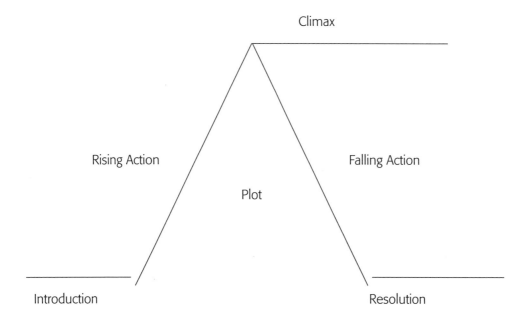

Epilogue

Remember Rocky? He was the "either-or" kid in Chapter 1 who had trouble in school from the day he entered pre-school. He is the subject of a typical tale told in faculty gatherings in every school every year. Rocky did survive and did increase the promise for a productive and happy life for himself, because many of his teachers added a few R's to their teaching and interactions with Rocky.

First, his fifth-grade teacher decided to put on a class play. Being the class clown, Rocky was a natural for the lead which required use of his intelligence and his comfort in "acting out" in front of others. Structuring his actions to fit into something productive and appreciated by others opened new types of expectations for Rocky. This teacher recognized Rocky's talent and that RECOGNITION OF TALENT is another inroad to student success.

Rocky had such success with the acting experience in a simple classroom play, that he sought other ways to use his talents positively. He had a leading role in the middle school play each year and by high school was known as the kid who could sing, dance, and act. His work on many aspects of the high school musicals led him to a college scholarship in theater where he found a real passion for puppetry and he eventually went to work in New York.

Recognition of talent is often difficult in classrooms where the focus is on the development of only reading, math, or writing skills. Students who have strengths in physical, interpersonal, artistic, or other areas of intelligence are rarely given opportunities to show what they have learned using their strengths.

Schools that have opportunities for students to explore and develop their talents in areas outside of the standard curriculum will have fewer at-risk students. Middle and high schools that provide opportunities for students to use their talents in culinary, health occupations, mechanics, construction, performing and studio arts, business, and technology will keep more kids interested in coming to school and completing their coursework. One student remarked, "Why do they call art a minor subject when it's the major love of my life?" (Ricken, p. 8) Unfortunately, as these programs decrease, the dropout rate increases and those who do not understand the nature and needs of the at-risk students offer them only more of the same that has caused them to fail in the first place. The Rockys of the world do not always fit into the standard system, but can be educated to provide essential skills and services to their communities.

In addition to recognition of talent, Rocky's teachers also used RELE-VANCE in the curriculum that they taught. Examples used to clarify material, problems generated in math, writing assignments in language arts, social studies issues, and science experiments were all current and related to the lives of the students. Students in our study told us that they wanted to know *why* they had to learn the "stuff" being thrown at them. Learning information for an upcoming test does not provide incentive to those who question the system and their role in schools. Savvy educators ask themselves the question, "Why is it important for my students to learn this information," and they relay that rationale to their students. If the teachers can find no relevance, they talk with other teachers about the curriculum, bring it up at faculty and curriculum meetings, and insure that what they are teaching really does matter. So often we add, add, add to the curriculum and list of learning expectations, but rarely do we cull it for relevance. It's time to do so. Often the relevance is found in a topic's REAL WORLD application. Measurement is used when designing a ball field, democratic principles are used in classroom meetings, persuasive techniques are applied in letters written to administrators in support of food choices offered in the cafeteria. There is no question that the curriculum in America's schools needs to be studied in each local entity. Connections need to be made among the subject areas more efficiently to meet standards and to demonstrate to students how problems are solved using various perspectives.

And finally, REFLECTION needs to be taught and practiced for use by students *and* adults. Learning occurs when we take the time to think about the new information presented and how it fits, or doesn't fit, into our existing schema. We've known that for years, but we have become so distracted by time on task and efficiency, that we have thrown the baby out with the bathwater. What is not reflected upon is forgotten. We each need time to wrestle with new ideas, talk with others about them, and try them out in practical ways. As you finish reading this book, take time to reflect on its meaning in your own context. Talk with your colleagues about it. And remember, if you reach one troubled student and help them to reduce their risk and increase their promise, you have earned your salary in spades. We wish you luck and thank you for your dedication to helping those who need us the most.

Reference

Ricken, R. (1987). *Love me when I'm most unlovable*, Book two: The kids' view. Reston, VA: National Association of Secondary School Principals, p. 8.

Notes

Notes